## What others are saying about *Journey with Bunyan's Pilgrim*

Thanks to Ann Coker for providing a helpful guide for bringing this age-old classic to the modern Sunday school class, small group, book club, or personal study. Pilgrim's lessons are as relevant today as they were in 1678!

—James N. Watkins, award-winning author and speaker

I loved going through this journey with the author, her insights, and her evident faith. The book includes concise summaries, clear connections to Scripture and biblical truths, and relevant takeaways with thought-invoking questions. This companion book will be a great asset to anyone who wants to get the most out of reading Bunyan's *The Pilgrim's Progress*.

—Kim Van Ee, ESL instructor and fellow pilgrim

Years ago, I enjoyed reading John Bunyan's *The Pilgrim's Progress*. Ann's *Journey with Bunyan's Pilgrim* encourages us to reflect on personal choices, focus, and perseverance. The goal? A more intimate relationship with God. A journey worth taking; the Celestial City awaits.

—Joyce Long, author of *Real Mothers: Bible study about mothers for mothers* and *Trinity: Walk in Love, Forgiveness and Peace*

It's difficult to express how much I have appreciated Ann Coker through the years for her faithful encouragement and witness to the truth of the Gospel of Jesus Christ. And now she brings her gentle spirit and wise counsel to the pages of a new work. Anyone who loves the classic *The Pilgrim's Progress* is going to be thrilled with this insightful companion guide.

—Peter Heck, preaching minister,
Jerome Christian Church

A classic within a classic, *Journey with Bunyan's Pilgrim* is full of insightful applications encouraging us to dig deeper into the timeless allegory and more importantly even deeper into God's Word. Journaling will personalize Christian's walk and strengthen your faith.

—Beth Summitt, author, speaker,
Vice President of Real Faith Ministries

The only thing better than reading John Bunyan's classic is reading it with a guide that helps you process and integrate the timeless wisdom in its pages. Ann Coker has provided such a guide, structured as a 13-week journey that's both enlightening and inspiring. In fact, Ann's book is more than a guide; it's an invitation to explore, reflect and embark on a transformative journey. Godspeed!

—Chad R. Allen, writing coach for BookCamp
and author of *Do Your Art*

What a privilege it was to read Ann's book. I thoroughly enjoyed seeing how she brought everything together—her thoughts and Bunyan's original approach.

—Ethel Kearns Mayer, retired high school English teacher

Ann Coker's *Journey with Bunyan's Pilgrim* serves the reader like no other devotional I've ever experienced. Instead of direct Bible study with applicable questions over the Scripture passage, Coker begins with a snippet from *The Pilgrim's Progress*, then points to Scripture that applies to the story. A refreshing reversal! In two pages each day, she develops a powerful lesson and challenges readers to reflect on their own relationship with the King of Kings as they journey to their eternal home.

—Linda Sammaritan, author of *World Without Sound* series and blogger www.lindasammaritan.com

In *Journey with Bunyan's Pilgrim*, Ann Coker has written a wonderful, practical guide to help readers tap even deeper into the richness of Bunyan's classic, *The Pilgrim's Progress*. For over three centuries untold thousands have had their lives changed by what is arguably one of the most significant books ever written. Now, in *Journey with Bunyan's Pilgrim*, Ann will help you journal through Bunyan's masterpiece so you can add your name to the ever-growing list of grateful pilgrims whose lives have been forever impacted by it.

—Mike Spencer, Project LifeVoice

Because of Ann's format, the book can be used as an effective guide for small group study. Members would be exposed to a classic in literature, to Scripture that directs the life of a Christian, to a witness of His grace, and to the practice of keeping a journal to record God's love as we progress as pilgrims in a weary land, longing for Bunyan's "celestial city" whose builder and maker is God.

—Yvonne Moulton, retired professor of English, Asbury University

# Journey with Bunyan's Pilgrim

# Journey with Bunyan's Pilgrim

A Companion Guide for *The Pilgrim's Progress*

## Ann L. Coker

Foreword by Yvonne Moulton

**EABooks Publishing**
Your Partner In Publishing

*Journey with Bunyan's Pilgrim*
Copyright © 2023 Ann L. Coker

All rights reserved. No part of this publication may be reproduced, distributed, or transmitted in any form or by any means, without prior written permission.

*The Pilgrim's Progress*, John Bunyan (Parts I and II), edition with Scripture references & notes by Bunyan, complete and unabridged, The Christian Library © 1998. Published by Barbour and Company, Inc., Westwood, NJ. ISBN 0-916441-00-8

*The Pilgrim's Progress,* John Bunyan, Updated in Today's Language, Abridged Christian Classics, © 2010 by Barbour Publishing, Inc. ISBN 978-1-60260-853-5

Unless otherwise indicated, all scripture quotations are taken from THE HOLY BIBLE, NEW INTERNATIONAL VERSION®, NIV® Copyright © 1973, 1978, 1984, 2011 by Biblica, Inc.™ Used by permission. All rights reserved worldwide.

*Journey with Bunyan's Pilgrim*
by Ann L. Coker

ISBN: 978-1-955309-70-7
LCCN: 2023918941

EABooks Publishing
www.eabookspublishing.com

Dedicated to

Dr. William B. Coker, Sr.,
my husband and pastor.
He has led me and traveled with me
on life's journey
for over sixty-six years.

# Table of Contents

Foreword by Yvonne Moulton ........................................ 1
Synopsis of *The Pilgrim's Progress* ................................. 3
Introduction ............................................................... 5
Journaling .................................................................. 7

**Part I: Christian Journeys to the Celestial City**
**Week 1: Pilgrim Left Home**
    Day 1 – What Shall I Do? ..................................... 10
    Day 2 – Though None Go with Me ..................... 12
    Day 3 – Two Faces of Resolve .............................. 14
    Day 4 – Help Is at Hand ....................................... 16
    Day 5 – Meanwhile Back Home ......................... 18
    Day 6 – Choose the Best Over the Good .......... 20

**Week 2: At the Cross**
    Day 1 – Shame Can Be Good .............................. 22
    Day 2 – The Gate Is Open to Sinners ................ 24
    Day 3 – Rooms for Interpretation ..................... 26
    Day 4 – Cross and Sepulcher .............................. 28
    Day 5 – The Lost Is Found .................................. 30
    Day 6 – From Where and To Where ................. 32

## Week 3: Prepared for Battle
- Day 1 – Table Talk .................. 34
- Day 2 – Persuaded to Stay .................. 36
- Day 3 – Victory Over the Enemy .................. 38
- Day 4 – Light Within Shadows .................. 40
- Day 5 – A Faithful Companion .................. 42
- Day 6 – Much Talk, No Power .................. 44

## Week 4: Early Entrance to Heaven
- Day 1 – A Prophet's Preparation .................. 46
- Day 2 – Entering Vanity Fair .................. 48
- Day 3 – Prosecutor's Witnesses .................. 50
- Day 4 – Faithful's Defense .................. 52
- Day 5 – Jury's Verdict .................. 54
- Day 6 – Transported .................. 56

## Week 5: Good and Bad Company
- Day 1 – Hopeful Joined Christian .................. 58
- Day 2 – Rich Friends in Fair-speech .................. 60
- Day 3 – What Gain for What Reason? .................. 62
- Day 4 – Come and See .................. 64
- Day 5 – Remember Lot's Wife .................. 66
- Day 6 – The Way Back .................. 68

## Week 6: Doubt Led to Despair
- Day 1 – Doubting Castle .................. 70
- Day 2 – Giant Despair and His Wife .................. 72
- Day 3 – What Shall We Do? .................. 74
- Day 4 – Hopeful Lived Up to His Name .................. 76
- Day 5 – Remember Past Victories .................. 78
- Day 6 – Key of Promise .................. 80

**Week 7: Beware of Shortcuts**
- Day 1 – Escaped and Refreshed ......................... 82
- Day 2 – Within Sight of the City ....................... 84
- Day 3 – Shepherds Lead ..................................... 86
- Day 4 – The Way of Understanding ................. 88
- Day 5 – Clear Perspective ................................... 90
- Day 6 – Secrets and Warnings .......................... 92

**Week 8: Snared by Flattery**
- Day 1 – Ignorance Added Nothing .................... 94
- Day 2 – Little-Faith ............................................... 96
- Day 3 – Great-Grace ............................................. 98
- Day 4 – Flatterers ................................................ 100
- Day 5 – Hopeful's Testimony ........................... 102
- Day 6 – Good Use of Fear ................................. 104

**Week 9: Sweet Beulah Land**
- Day 1 – Sunshine Night and Day .................... 106
- Day 2 – Sick with Love ...................................... 108
- Day 3 – Through the River ............................... 110
- Day 4 – Wedding Supper with Jesus .............. 112
- Day 5 – Welcomed Home .................................. 114
- Day 6 – Way to Hell ............................................ 116

**Part II: Christiana Journeys to the Celestial City**

**Week 10: The Following**
- Day 1 – Packed to Go ......................................... 120
- Day 2 – Mercy Came .......................................... 122
- Day 3 – Follow His Example ............................ 124
- Day 4 – The Way In ............................................ 126
- Day 5 – Forbidden Fruit ................................... 128
- Day 6 – Christiana's Guilt ................................ 130

## Week 11: Consequences and Victories
- Day 1 – Privileged Place ........................ 132
- Day 2 – Creatures and Flowers ............... 134
- Day 3 – Bathed and Clothed .................. 136
- Day 4 – Pardon by Another .................... 138
- Day 5 – Gave an Account ....................... 140
- Day 6 – No Thought to Retreat .............. 142

## Week 12: It's Not All Up-hill
- Day 1 – Lover of Pilgrims ....................... 144
- Day 2 – Favored Women and Weddings ......... 146
- Day 3 – Food and Riddles........................ 148
- Day 4 – Feeble-mind and Ready-to-Halt ........ 150
- Day 5 – The End of Giant Despair ............ 152
- Day 6 – Ask and Receive ......................... 154

## Week 13: Valiant-for-truth
- Day 1 – Sword of Truth .......................... 156
- Day 2 – Shall We Know One Another? ........ 158
- Day 3 – Rehearsals ................................. 160
- Day 4 – Light the Way ............................ 162
- Day 5 – Blessings and Bequeaths .............. 164
- Day 6 – Journey's End ............................ 166

**Conclusion: Where Do We Go from Here?** ......... 168

**Resources as Endnotes** ............................... 171

**Acknowledgements** ..................................... 175

**About the Author** ....................................... 177

# Foreword

*The Pilgrim's Progress* by John Bunyan has been my long-time friend. Recently I found an old copy on the second row of my bookshelf, behind books I read or use more often. I also saw it frequently because my special-needs son pulled *his* pictorial tattered copy off *his* bookshelf and began to go through it again. Kevin often stopped at the cross, relieved that Christian had lost his burden, the bundle on his back.

Bunyan has done for Kevin what Ann Coker does in her devotional book—brings God and Bunyan's story into reality and makes them one's own experience. Paralleling Bunyan's narrative with Scripture, most of which is found in the margins of some of the Bunyan editions, Ann interweaves parts of her own story which is written from her long spiritual discipline of journaling. She demonstrates how much the allegory describes the journey of the Christian, both its triumphs, its downfalls, and temptations. She punctuates, as does Bunyan, the reality of God's promise that He is faithful and "will not allow you to be tempted beyond what you are able, but with the temptation will provide the way of escape" (1 Corinthians 10:13, NASB).

Because of her format, the book can be used by individuals, but also as an effective guide for small group study. Members would be exposed to a classic in literature, to Scripture that directs the life of a Christian, to a witness of His grace, and to the practice of keeping a journal to record God's love as we progress as pilgrims in a weary land, longing for Bunyan's "celestial city" whose builder and maker is God.

—**Yvonne Moulton**
Retired Professor of English, Asbury University, Wilmore, Kentucky

# Synopsis of
# *The Pilgrim's Progress*
# by John Bunyan

John Bunyan (1628–1688) wrote *The Pilgrim's Progress* while in prison in Bedford, England. Since its first publication in 1678, millions have read this allegory for its beauty and simplicity about a Christian's life journey. Besides its endurance, this book is a classic because readers apply its truths to their own spiritual journeys.

Some people start reading Bunyan's book and don't finish. If it's due to the 17th century English, the modern language editions eliminate that reason. Editions for children have also been published, as well as versions in audio and visual formats. Other readers don't connect with the allegory, but deep meanings behind the characters and situations blend their stories into ours.

The most important element of Bunyan's work is how he infuses Scripture into his allegory. In both unabridged and modern editions, biblical references abound to connect readers with the truths of life's journey. Some modern editions even include explanatory notes on vocabulary and historical facts to enhance readers' understanding.

The main character, Christian, begins his journey by leaving his town of Destruction. Evangelist guides him to the Cross, where his burden of sin rolls off his back into a sealed tomb. Along the Way he meets people who either help or hinder his travel to the Celestial City. The names of these characters reflect their inner strength or weakness; such examples include Faithful and Hopeful as well as Pliable and Lord Hate-good. Christian's walk is not easy, for while others may hinder him, he must also deal with his own faults, such as pride and doubt.

Christian does reach the Celestial City with his friend Hopeful. Soon to follow him are his wife, Christiana, and their four sons, in part two of Bunyan's book. While their journeys are different, motives and results exhibit goodness. This story is not only theirs but ours.

# Introduction

From the subtitle for John Bunyan's classic, *The Pilgrim's Progress*, we read "from this world to that which is to come." The author set out to establish a connection between here and there, from now and into the future. A certain man went on a dangerous journey, intending to have a "safe arrival at the desired country."* Bunyan stated that his work was about a dream, but truly it is a look into real life for anyone seeking to experience the Christian walk.

Many books are available to expound on John Bunyan's life and his works. Each has its own purpose. My intent in writing is personal. Having read *The Pilgrim's Progress* many times, I rate it next after the Bible as my most valued book for the Christian life. Not only is Bunyan's work a literary classic, it connects a study in Scripture with personal Christian experience. While opening chapters dwell on the evangelistic aspects of the pilgrim, the meeting at the cross and subsequent travels highlight the walk of anyone's Christian faith.

My own personal journey in faith involves connections. Relating Scripture to personal life is vastly more important than we give this process credit. That is why I connect Pilgrim's journey with Bunyan's Scripture references and my own personal walk.

As you take this journey with Pilgrim you may also journal in order to connect with Scripture references. Prepare yourself. On this route you'll meet obstacles, snags, and people who won't support you, but you will also have rewarding fellowship with some special travelers.

Daily entries are staged as devotions, quoting from Bunyan, citing Scripture references, followed by personal reflections found in my journals. I invite you to journal alongside Bunyan's Pilgrim. I've used Barbour's 1998 edition of *The Pilgrim's Progress*, so page numbers reflect that book. Many editions are available for your use. You may even have one on your bookshelf.

*1998 Christian Library Edition, *The Pilgrim's Progress*, permission by Barbour Publishing Inc., Uhrichsville, OH

# Journaling

I find journaling to be a good creative exercise, an expression and reflection on what I've read, thought, and done. As to whom I'm writing in my journal, that's still up for grabs. Sometimes my entries are prayers or close to it, and at times I may be writing to another person who will someday read my journal. More often than not, I'm writing for my own benefit. Putting it down on paper helps sort out my thoughts, evaluate my attitudes and actions, and give the subject a chance to expand and connect.

As previously said, connections are a big part of why I write, especially as I bring two or more passages of Scripture together or as I connect my life with God and His Word. Looking back over my journals through the years, I discover the purpose of my life's journey.

For me journaling is a means of expressing love and hope, but also fear and doubt. I can be honest on a blank page. Journaling brings my life into proper focus—to be a positive influence on myself and others, to be light in darkness.

In my journals, I bring the past and present together and even speak into the future. I express myself best on paper. Perhaps it's because writing is a medium to give me time to think. I reflect and set patterns, make decisions, and notice how my faith works.

Unless I am changed, life experiences are of no value. I must bear the mark of the disposition of Christ, following His example of servanthood and *being* His epistle.

As you travel with Bunyan's pilgrim, Christian, you are given opportunity to journal. The format of this book is meant to be one of connecting your life with Scripture as Christian journeys to the Celestial City. Let's travel there together.

Part I

# Christian Journeys to the Celestial City

## Week One: Pilgrim Left Home

# "What Shall I Do?"

## WEEK ONE DAY ONE

"I saw a Man clothed with rags...a Book in his hand, and a great Burden upon his back" (p. 1).

"All of us have become like one who is unclean, and all our righteous acts are like filthy rags" (Isaiah 64:6, NIV 2011). "Peter replied, 'Repent and be baptized, every one of you, in the name of Jesus Christ for the forgiveness of your sins'" (Acts 2:38).

John Bunyan opened his narrative with a dream. He saw a man reading a Book, weeping because of a great burden on his back. The man cried out, "What shall I do?" Although his conviction of sin resulted from reading the book, the book also contained the remedy: "Repent."

Pilgrim neither wanted to die nor face the judgment. But something must be done. What? Evangelist was appointed to guide him. Ahead lay a gate that doesn't come into view until light shines upon it. God's Word is this light (Psalm 119:105).

God's Word is truly a double-edged sword (Hebrews 4:12), for while it admonishes us about sin, it also shows us the way to be rid of sin (Romans 5:21). Evangelist led Pilgrim to the light. We all need qualified leaders equipped with biblical truth.

**My Takeaway:** I am thankful for my Sunday school teacher who gave the opportunity for high-school students to make a personal decision for Christ. She took this invitation seriously, for she even withheld her own pre-teen son from joining the church after attending membership class. Being a Christ-follower has more eternal weight than being a church member.

**Your Turn:** How were you introduced to biblical truth?

................................................................
................................................................
................................................................
................................................................
................................................................
................................................................
................................................................
................................................................

# Though None Go with Me

## WEEK ONE DAY TWO

"Now he had not run far from his own door, but his wife and children perceiving it, began to cry after him to return" (p. 4).

"As soon as they [the angels] had brought them out, one of them said, 'Flee for your lives! Don't look back, and don't stop anywhere in the plain!'" (Genesis 19:17).

Pilgrim's hometown would soon be destroyed, so he pled with his wife and children to escape with him. Instead, his family and friends grew convinced he was mad. Determined in his resolve, Pilgrim cried out, "Life! Life! Eternal life!" and did not look back as he fled.

This scene was based on Lot's exit from Sodom and the warning the angels gave his family. It also introduced the cost of discipleship. If we are not willing to leave mother and father, wife and children, any family member, we cannot follow Christ. (See Luke 14: 26, 27.)

Pilgrim saw the grim reality of what his decision meant to leave a city in ruins, but his main concern focused on salvation, safety now and for eternity. He decided to leave home in search of redemption, as he invited those whom he loved. When none would go with Pilgrim, it came to the parting of their ways.

**My Takeaway:** A seminary student served my husband and me a simple meal, but his testimony became the main course. He had come from an Asian country to Kentucky USA for ministerial studies, and at quite a cost. He no longer had family, for once he declared his allegiance to Christ, his parents disowned him. In a personal way, he introduced me to the persecuted church.

**Your Turn:** Was your conversion viewed by family with joy or disdain? How did that affect your commitment?

..............................................................................................

..............................................................................................

..............................................................................................

..............................................................................................

..............................................................................................

..............................................................................................

..............................................................................................

..............................................................................................

..............................................................................................

# Two Faces of Resolve

## WEEK ONE DAY THREE

"There were two that were resolved to fetch him back by force. The name of the one was Obstinate, and the name of the other Pliable" (p. 4).

"But since they have no root, they last only a short time. When trouble or persecution comes because of the word, they quickly fall away" (Matthew 13:21).

Two neighbors, Obstinate and Pliable, decided to follow Pilgrim with the intent to force him to return home. Up to this point we know Pilgrim only as "the Man," but when he answered their inquiry, his true name surfaced—Christian. As with all of Bunyan's characters, names reveal their inner nature. Bunyan explained that Christian sought an incorruptible inheritance. Obstinate would have none of it, and he pulled in the opposite direction, begging Pliable to return with him. But Pliable was curious enough to go a little way with Christian, attracted by the pleasantries of a kingdom, crowns, and shining garments.

Distracted while talking, the two travelers fell heedlessly into the Slough of Despond. Ah, this became the dividing of wills, for Pliable saw this way brought no quick and easy happiness. He got out of the slough [deep bog, marsh] on the side next to his house and left.

**My Takeaway:** While Obstinate was set in his way, unwilling to listen to Christian's resolve, Pliable was without any root, much like the seed planted in rocky soil. He saw joy at first, but when trouble came, he revealed neither readiness nor ability to learn and grow. I've found a consistent devotional life takes a resolve of intentional living. That means being rooted in the Word, for then negatives are weeded out and positive nutrients added on a daily basis.

**Your Turn:** What does "Slough of Despond" mean to you personally?

...........................................................................................
...........................................................................................
...........................................................................................
...........................................................................................
...........................................................................................
...........................................................................................
...........................................................................................

# Help Is at Hand

## WEEK ONE DAY FOUR

"But why did you not look for the Steps?" (p. 9). "When I was in great need, he saved me" (Psalm 116:6).

Scholars acclaim Bunyan's creation of the Slough of Despond as his best contribution to the book's images met along the Christian walk. It's a vivid picture of Psalm 40:2 where David praised God: "He lifted me out of the slimy pit, out of the mud and mire; he set my feet on a rock and gave me a firm place to stand."

When navigating the slough, Christian had more difficulty than Pliable because of the burden on his back. At the same time, he moved to the side further away from his home, showing a commitment to seek salvation. When he most needed it, someone came to his aid. Help asked why he was there, directed him to the steps, and reached out his hand. Help bid him to continue on his way. But first Christian was curious about the Slough of Despond and why it had been placed along the Way to the gate.

**My Takeaway:** Pilgrim's question is also one I might ask. Why would such a place of mud and mire be left to hinder a Christian along the way of salvation? The answer Bunyan gave by way of Help can be borne out in my own experience. Fears, doubts, and discouragement have risen in my mind during those times when the Holy Spirit convicted of sin. But help was found when I asked for it. The Rock of Ages lifted me onto solid ground. Knowing such truth has brought comfort indeed, and questioning the way of Christian faith provided wisdom. Asking for help hasn't slowed down my process but instead given answers to speed me on my way.

**Your Turn:** Give names to the "steps" one should take to be saved.

.................................................................................

.................................................................................

.................................................................................

.................................................................................

.................................................................................

.................................................................................

.................................................................................

.................................................................................

.................................................................................

.................................................................................

# Meanwhile Back Home
## WEEK ONE DAY FIVE

"By this time Pliable got home to his house again" (p. 10).

"Strengthen the feeble hands, steady the knees that give way; say to those with fearful hearts, 'Be strong, do not fear'" (Isaiah 35:3–4).

Pliable arrived home and his curious neighbors greeted him. Pliable became their subject as some threw gibes and others gave compliments. Some called him wise; others said he was a fool for even going that far with Christian. Still more even named him a coward for giving up after "a few difficulties." True to his name, Pliable deflected the insults toward Christian, getting friends off his back and onto the pilgrim who had left town.

Unaware of all the talk back home, Christian was alone on his journey. Both neighbors had left, and Evangelist and Help no longer traveled with him. Their part seemed to be over in preparing Christian for his journey toward the gate, the Way to salvation.

The Old Testament records that the Israelites asked Samuel to pray for them, for they feared they had sinned when asking for a king. The people went directly to their priest, but unlike Pliable, they did not talk behind his back. Samuel went so far as to call not praying a sin. Then he added, "I will teach you the way that is good and right" (I Samuel 12:23).

**My Takeaway:** At the office I found myself hard pressed to befriend a co-worker. My solution? I kept an envelope in my desk drawer and slipped in a small note when I noticed something I appreciated about her. Those notes, seen only by me, made a difference in our relationship. This practical activity also kept me from bad-mouthing my co-worker to others.

**Your Turn:** Relate a time when you have stood alone.

# Choosing the Best over the Good

WEEK ONE DAY SIX

Worldly Wiseman said, "The remedy is at hand. Besides, I will add, that instead of these dangers, thou shalt meet with much safety, friendship, and content" (p. 13).

"For the wisdom of this world is foolishness in God's sight. As it is written: 'He catches the wise in their craftiness'" (1 Corinthians 3:19).

Master Worldly Wiseman met up with Christian, and their looks and demeanor contrast. Bunyan introduced Worldly Wiseman as a gentleman, clothed in fine raiment, while Christian carried a heavy bundle of rags upon his back. The conversation began with questions about Christian's family. Because of his burden, Christian felt like he had no family. Worldly Wiseman asked about his awful load and then proposed another plan: Christian could go into the village of Morality and there find Legality and Civility to help with his burden.

This suggestion promised safety, friendship, and contentment, but were they the best for

Christian's plight? He must choose between what seemed good and the best. The world appreciates such qualities, and that's the point. If we depend on our own morals, what's legal and civil, we get by. But do we know God's grace which brings salvation through Christ's sacrifice? Christian started up the hill to Legality's house, and the way grew hard and his burden heavier.

**My Takeaway:** Counseling at a crisis pregnancy center, I met women and men who chose the wrong way to satisfy their basic human urges. Led by the Spirit, peer-counselors offered them God's way. In my own testimony I was the "good little girl"—but not saved. My good life (the self-righteous way) could be likened to filthy rags until I, like Pilgrim, came to the cross.

**Your Turn:** Describe the difference between worldly and godly wisdom.

................................................................
................................................................
................................................................
................................................................
................................................................
................................................................
................................................................
................................................................

## Week Two: At the Cross

# Shame Can Be Good
## WEEK TWO DAY ONE

Christian "saw Evangelist coming to meet him; at the sight also of whom he began to blush for Shame." . . . Evangelist "began to reason with Christian" (p. 15).

"Come now, and let us reason together, saith the Lord" (Isaiah 1:18, KJV).

At the sight of Evangelist, Christian blushed with shame. Evangelist questioned Christian who at first defended his departure from the prescribed Way to the Wicket Gate. The advice of Worldly Wiseman seemed at first to be good, or at least easy. However, Christian found no relief from his burden.

Evangelist's reasoning counteracted the worldly wisdom that led Christian astray. From this experience Christian learned to hate three things: if he turned out of the Way, if the Cross seemed too hard, and if someone persuaded him to take the path of death. The emphasis remained on the Cross—to prefer that more than any treasures he could collect. All Evangelist's teaching was saturated with Scripture from the Gospels and Epistles. "May I never boast except in the cross of our Lord Jesus Christ" (Galatians 6:14).

Christian asked if he still had any hope. Evangelist neither ignored nor excused the pilgrim's sin, but instead sent him on his way to the gate. Determination now ruled his steps.

**My Takeaway:** Christian's sorrow led to repentance. At first shame is defined as something damaging, but shame can lead to confession and redemption. If I admit my shameful acts, I start the road to recovery and then I can right the wrong. I'm grateful for second chances, for even now as a great-grandma, I need hope for today's failures and tomorrow's fears.

**Your Turn:** What second chance has God given you by His grace?

..................................................................................
..................................................................................
..................................................................................
..................................................................................
..................................................................................
..................................................................................

# The Gate Is Open to Sinners
## WEEK TWO DAY TWO

"So in the process of time Christian got up to the Gate" (p. 20).

"Strait is the gate, and narrow is the way, which leadeth unto life" (Matthew 7:14a, KJV).

Walking with caution, Christian reached the Wicket Gate. As instructed, he knocked and Goodwill came asking his purpose for being there. Christian identified himself as a "burdened sinner." However, none of Christian's faults cast him out (John 6:37). With that confession, Goodwill opened the gate and pulled him inside. Nearby stood the strong castle of Beelzebub who shot arrows of deception at those entering the gate.

Goodwill gave Christian opportunity to rehearse his journey thus far. In due time Goodwill showed Christian the narrow Way and warned him of strangers and difficulties he would meet. Burdened by the load of sins on his back, Christian sought to be rid of it. Goodwill assured him that the burden would fall off by itself at the place of deliverance.

**My Takeaway:** Our physical birthing process takes time. But too often I want or even labor to rush the spiritual birth of someone I care about. Christian's route to where his burden falls off was fraught with delays and pitfalls. For him to reach the place of deliverance took valuable time. Goodwill warned Christian that every turn from the Way would be crooked and wide. The right Way is straight and narrow. Not something I want to hear, for too often I would choose my own way. Those times when I've said no to God have resulted in my running into crooked, sharp turns which led me away from what God has called me to be.

**Your Turn:** How should you, a Christian, select the right way? What might get in your way?

...........................................................................
...........................................................................
...........................................................................
...........................................................................
...........................................................................
...........................................................................
...........................................................................
...........................................................................
...........................................................................
...........................................................................

# Rooms for Interpretation
## WEEK TWO DAY THREE

"I am what I was not once.... I am now a man of Despair, and am shut up in it, as in this Iron Cage. I cannot get out" (p. 32).

"It is impossible for those who have . . . tasted the goodness of the word of God . . . and who have fallen away, to be brought back to repentance" (Hebrews 6:4–6).

Christian reached the House of the Interpreter, and the host opened several rooms, each intended to offer instruction for his journey. The occupant of one room alarmed Christian who asked how this man became caged. The man was forthright with his own confession: he grieved the Holy Spirit and knew that this promised him no chance of repentance. He enjoyed worldly pleasures instead of the goodness of God. As Christian left the house, he affirmed the lessons as either hopeful or fearful, but they all helped him better understand the Way.

Many have written about the idea of selling one's soul to the devil. Two you could check out are Christopher Marlowe's *Dr. Faustus* and Louisa May Alcott's *A Modern Mephistopheles*.

**My Takeaway:** In this illustration of the caged man, we are also introduced to an aspect of Bunyan's theology. An old hymn cites an invisible line that is drawn—the point where one is no longer convicted by the Holy Spirit. That line may connect with the verse about the unforgivable sin. Scholars believe this sin is against the Holy Spirit. "Do not grieve the Holy Spirit of God, with whom you were sealed for the day of redemption" (Ephesians 4:30). While mystery surrounds this Scripture, I do know how to escape the judgment and keep my salvation. If my heart and mind stay fixed on Jesus, I have personal assurance of salvation. (See Hebrews 12:1–3.)

**Your Turn:** What does selling your soul mean, and what prescription could you take against it?

..........................................................................................
..........................................................................................
..........................................................................................
..........................................................................................
..........................................................................................
..........................................................................................
..........................................................................................
..........................................................................................

# Cross and Sepulcher
## WEEK TWO DAY FOUR

"As Christian came up to the Cross, his burden loosed from off his shoulders" (p. 35).

"While we were still sinners, Christ died for us" (Romans 5:8), and "he has taken it [sin] away, nailing it to the cross" (Colossians 2:14).

Because of the burden on his back, Christian had difficulty climbing the hill of Calvary where he reached the Cross. Immediately his burden fell off and rolled into the tomb below, sealed forever. He received rest, exchanging sorrow for joy and death for life. Three Shining Ones greeted him with gifts: peace, forgiveness, a new robe, and a sealed scroll. They placed a mark on his forehead, and he sang: "Blest be the Man who was put to shame for me!"

At the bottom of the hill Christian awakened three men, bound in chains. Simple, Sloth, and Presumption saw no reason to struggle up the hill. Two other men, Formalist and Hypocrisy, climbed over a wall, and avoided the Gate. They offered an excuse: "What does it matter which way we get in?" Christian considered them as thieves who dishonored the Master of the Way. As they reached the Hill of Difficulty, Christian drank from a spring before ascending the hill. The other two men opted for what looked like easier routes but ended in danger and destruction.

**My Takeaway:** One evening at summer youth camp, I went forward to dedicate my life for Christian service. But later, on the top bunk in my cabin, the Lord convicted me of my sins, especially my habit of stretching the truth, which is really lying. I confessed and Jesus forgave me. My good intentions amounted to nothing but filthy rags. God exchanged them for His robe of righteousness and a new life.

**Your Turn:** What does the Cross of Christ mean to you?

..................................................................................
..................................................................................
..................................................................................
..................................................................................
..................................................................................
..................................................................................
..................................................................................
..................................................................................
..................................................................................

# The Lost Is Found

WEEK TWO DAY FIVE

"He asked God forgiveness for his foolish act, and then went back to look for his Scroll" (p. 43).

"You are all children of the light and children of the day" (1 Thessalonians 5:5). "You must be on your guard" (Mark 13:9).

Alongside the Hill of Difficulty an arbor provided some needed rest for weary pilgrims. But Christian slept too long. Then from two men going down the hill Christian learned of two lions that scared them. Still Christian ventured forward, but he was unaware that his scroll had fallen while sleeping. The scroll held instructions worthy for any traveler of the Way.

This loss caused Christian much distress for he needed comfort found in the scroll. Both guilt and fear—guilt for his misdeed and fear of the lions ahead—moved him to ask God's forgiveness, and it was freely given.

After retracing his steps to retrieve his scroll, Christian saw the Palace Beautiful and the two lions guarding the entrance. Watchful, the porter, assured him the lions were chained and Christian only had to walk in the middle of the path. It was a matter of trust.

**My Takeaway:** Like Christian, we too often lose important items from either our hands or heads. We need to be constantly on guard concerning our salvation, planting God's Word in our minds. Too many mornings I've caught myself saying, "Oh, I wish I had not overslept!" My desire for a daily habit of Bible study and prayer means that decision begins the night before. Going to bed early enough for a good night's sleep, I get up early enough for my quiet time. I don't regret this discipline, for time with God is well spent. Good habits form a lifestyle of consistency.

**Your Turn:** When is your quiet time and how consistent are you?

............................................................................

............................................................................

............................................................................

............................................................................

............................................................................

............................................................................

............................................................................

# From Where and To Where?

## WEEK TWO DAY SIX

"I would fain be where I shall die no more, and with the Company that shall continually cry, Holy, Holy, Holy" (p. 51).

"Therefore God is not ashamed to be called their God, for he has prepared a city for them" (Hebrews 11:16).

It's discovered that the "law of the house" Beautiful (p. 47) dictated that a guest answer questions about where he has been and where he is going. Discretion first asked who Christian is and how he came to be in the Way. While supper preparations were underway, others in the family—Prudence, Piety, and Charity—occupied their time learning about Christian's journey.

A new element emerged about Christian's visit at the cross. He saw Christ as his crucified Lord, "bleeding upon a Tree" (p. 49). Christian hoped some day to see the living Christ.

**My Takeaway:** To me this section highlights the importance of remembrance in our own spiritual walk. Over and again the prophets in the Old

Testament invoked people to remember. This practice would be good for each of us today—to remember how God has led us along the Way. To give value to this concept of remembrance, read and pray through the Psalms.

A crucifix, almost three feet high, hung in my husband's study. People asked him why. He said without hesitation that the blood of Jesus has delivered us, and only Jesus makes us whole. We are all lost without Christ, and our morals are warped by sin. We have the privilege to point others to the crucified Christ who offers salvation. Christ has also promised hope for our future—to live with Him forever in His heavenly home.

**Your Turn:** From where have you come and where do you hope to go?

........................................................................

........................................................................

........................................................................

........................................................................

........................................................................

........................................................................

........................................................................

........................................................................

........................................................................

## Week Three: Prepared for Battle

# Table Talk

### WEEK THREE DAY ONE

"All their talk at the Table was about the Lord of the Hill" (p. 53).

"Jesus and his apostles reclined at the table. And he said to them, 'I have eagerly desired to eat this Passover with you before I suffer'" (Luke 22:14–15).

Pilgrim's suppertime at the house Beautiful resembles the Last Supper and Holy Communion. Their feast proved to be secondary to their conversation about the Lord. Charity posed a penetrating question to Pilgrim about his family and why they did not accompany him. Christian's explanation was fraught with passion for the souls of his family. He wept. Because Christian did warn and invite his family to join him, Charity assured him that he would not be held accountable for their sin (a reference to Ezekiel 3:19).

The group continued to lift up Jesus and how His death released the power of death over us.

When we partake of Holy Communion, we celebrate our Lord's death, remembering His perfect and sufficient sacrifice for the sins of the whole world, for you, for me.

**My Takeaway:** When our friend from Germany came to visit, she anticipated what she called "table talk." Usually over cups of tea, we gathered at the kitchen table, and she asked my husband and me anything she'd been pondering. Her questions, always biblically based, pointed either to a puzzling passage of Scripture, a relationship, or a situation at her university. This Q&A time revealed what had been on her mind and how dedicated she was to know the truth.

**Your Turn:** How does the Last Supper connect with the time when two disciples watched Jesus break bread in the village of Emmaus (Luke 24:30–32)?

..............................................................................
..............................................................................
..............................................................................
..............................................................................
..............................................................................
..............................................................................
..............................................................................
..............................................................................

# Persuaded to Stay
## WEEK THREE DAY TWO

"He got up to go forward, but they desired him to stay till the next day also" (p. 56).

"Put on the full armor of God, so that you can take your stand against the devil's schemes" (Ephesians 6:11).

Christian slept in the room called Peace, and the first morning he sang about being next door to heaven. His hosts showed him some genealogy, proof of Jesus being the Son of "the Ancient of Days" (Daniel 7:9). They also read how Christ's heroes stood strong for what's right, recorded for us in Hebrews 11. On the second day Christian visited the armory and noticed its abundant supply. Again they bid him stay another day to see the Delectable Mountains in Immanuel's Land. When he set out on his journey, he received a "sword, shield, helmet, breast-plate, all-prayer, and shoes that would not wear out" (p. 56; Ephesians 6:13–18).

Equipped to continue his journey, Christian headed down into the Valley of Humiliation and found it dangerous. A devilish creature, here named

Apollyon, met up with him. Christian determined not to go back. One simple reason: Christian had no armor for his back.

**My Takeaway:** One school year a young single mother and her two pre-teen children lived in our finished basement. Each morning they met in our dining room, preparing for the day by putting on their armor. Usually the girl would start reciting the Ephesians chapter six passage. By the time they got to the sword and helmet the boy became more excited about the imagery. Their mom would then pray for each child, inserting specifics about their day. Hearing them from the kitchen, I made my own application and rejoiced in God's provision.

**Your Turn:** What parts of Christian's armor do you need for your day and why?

...........................................................................
...........................................................................
...........................................................................
...........................................................................
...........................................................................
...........................................................................
...........................................................................
...........................................................................
...........................................................................

# Victory Over the Enemy
## WEEK THREE DAY THREE

"He resolved to venture, and stand his ground" (pp. 58–59).

"When the day of evil comes, you may be able to stand your ground, and after you have done everything, to stand" (Ephesians 6:13).

Apollyon's monstrous body was covered with scales. That was his pride! Bunyan's portrayal of Apollyon somewhat matched the Apostle John's description of the beast in the twelfth chapter of Revelation: "feet like those of a bear and a mouth like that of a lion" (v. 2). Apollyon sought to claim Christian as his own; but Christian, although afraid, stood his ground.

Their discourse centered on the wages of each master, and Christian gave an apt rebuttal: "Your wages are such as a man could not live on; 'for the wages of sin is death'" (p. 59, Romans 6:23). Christian did not back down. When accused of his faults and failings, Christian did not dismiss them. Instead he claimed pardon, giving allegiance to his true Master whose services and wages are honorable.

The physical battle started with the enemy first tossing a fiery dart, deflected by Christian's shield. More darts wounded Christian badly, but he gained courage from reciting Scripture. Apollyon flew away, physically wounded and defeated by Scripture.

**My Takeaway:** Christian used a good defense and offense against the destroyer of souls. First, he agreed with accusations as he pointed to Jesus and His mercy. Next he confronted Apollyon in the way of biblical holiness. Christian saw the end from the beginning. Too often we get impatient and lose sight of the end times when the King will come in His glory. His light then and now is our shield and strength. God's word is a light for our path (Psalm 119:105).

**Your Turn:** "Resist the devil, and he will flee" (James 4:7). How can you practice that today?

..............................................................................

..............................................................................

..............................................................................

..............................................................................

..............................................................................

..............................................................................

..............................................................................

..............................................................................

# Light Within Shadows
## WEEK THREE DAY FOUR

"The light of the day made [the dangers] conspicuous to him" (p. 69).

"Though I walk through the darkest valley, I will fear no evil, for you are with me" (Psalm 23:4).

The Way to the Celestial City lay through the midst of the Valley of the Shadow of Death, described by Jeremiah as "a land of drought and utter darkness, a land where no one travels and no one lives" (2:6). Even with these expected dangers, Christian must travel this way. Two men, going away from the valley, tried to dissuade Christian from entering. They described the horrific sights and sounds: "Death also doth always spread his wings over it" (p. 65).

Christian continued in the Way with his sword drawn. On the right side of the valley lay a ditch and on the left a quagmire, both covered in darkness. He exchanged his sword for another weapon: prayer. As he cried out to God, Christian remembered how he had already conquered many other dangers. Yet a subtle danger arose—internal whispers of condemnation. Sorting through this, he heard a voice quote the twenty-third Psalm. The sun broke through the shadows of darkness and revealed corpses of those who had earlier gone that way.

**My Takeaway:** When our daughter faced temptations to turn away from her Christian roots, the remembrance of our son's victory over his rebellious teen years sealed my hope for her future. Light shone through the darkness of doubt. Looking back, I knew God walked beside us, giving assurance of His peace. Our daughter is now a youth director's wife and joins him in ministry.

**Your Turn:** Describe a dark valley you have walked through and how God was with you. Perhaps it's a ripe time for you to claim hope for an oft-repeated prayer request.

..........................................................................................

..........................................................................................

..........................................................................................

..........................................................................................

..........................................................................................

..........................................................................................

..........................................................................................

..........................................................................................

# A Faithful Companion
## WEEK THREE DAY FIVE

"Looking forward, he saw Faithful before him upon his journey" (p. 71).

"So the last will be first, and the first will be last" (Matthew 20:16).

Christian saw Faithful ahead. It took a bit of doing for each to connect because Faithful did not want to delay his pilgrimage. Christian outran his hometown friend, then stumbled and fell due to his pride. Faithful helped him up and they walked on together. Here, as often in Bunyan's narrative, these pilgrims rehearsed the mishaps and success of their journeys.

While we know Christian's story, Faithful had different adventures. Drawn into Wanton's net of flattery, Faithful escaped, as did Joseph in the Genesis account (39:11–12). He recounted his time at the Hill of Difficulty and the Valley of Humility where he met Discontent.

Of all those whom Faithful met, one stood out as the most troublesome. His name was Shame; but Faithful said the name did not suit, for he was without shame. For example, Shame believed a person should not need to ask forgiveness from a neighbor or make restitution.

**My Takeaway:** Not all Christians have traveled the same path, but all of us know the love and strength of God's provision, protection, and presence. Having heart-to-heart conversations with Christian friends has given us different perspectives on how God brings us along our walk. I recall one meeting with a young mom as we combined breakfast, shopping, and prayer. Ours was an easy, no-pressure, honest relationship. With other friends I have shared a common interest in writing, yet our life journeys vary. With each friend I'm grown in my walk with the Lord.

**Your Turn:** How does your Christian experience differ from that of a close friend?

....................................................................................

....................................................................................

....................................................................................

....................................................................................

....................................................................................

....................................................................................

....................................................................................

....................................................................................

# Much Talk, No Power

## WEEK THREE DAY SIX

"Yea, if a man have all knowledge, he may yet be nothing; and so consequently be no child of God" (p. 90).

"For the kingdom of God is not a matter of talk but of power" (1 Corinthians 4:20).

Following at a short distance, another pilgrim joined Christian and Faithful. Entering eagerly into a conversation with Faithful, Talkative hoped it would be pleasant and profitable (p. 82). After such talk, Faithful asked Christian if he knew the man. Yes. Talkative had lived in Prating-Row, sporting a better reputation abroad than at home while he caused many to stumble and fall. Faithful confessed that this man had quickly deceived him. Thus, they devised a plan to have Talkative leave their company by his own will.

The plan worked, for it revealed Talkative's true nature. One topic contrasted people's reactions to sin: cry out against it or abhor it (p. 89). The biblical example showed how Potiphar's wife cried out to her household about Joseph's "sin." Talkative did not like this discourse about power and grace—to live the Word as well as know it—and so he left.

**My Takeaway:** In my early years as a Christian I thought I had to have something to say during discussions about biblical matters. I seldom said, "I don't know." Thus, my exposition gave evidence to my lack of true knowledge, sounding like a loud gong or tinkling cymbal (1 Corinthians 13:1). I like the rule one young Christian woman has adopted: "I don't expound on what I don't understand." That shows wisdom, the application of knowledge and understanding.

**Your Turn:** Have you ever found yourself talking too much about Christian beliefs with little knowledge to match your claim? Does your walk match your talk?

..........................................................................................

..........................................................................................

..........................................................................................

..........................................................................................

..........................................................................................

..........................................................................................

..........................................................................................

..........................................................................................

..........................................................................................

## Week Four: Early Entrance to Heaven

# A Prophet's Preparation
### WEEK FOUR DAY ONE

"He was a Prophet, and could tell them of things that might happen unto them, and also how they might resist and overcome them" (pp. 96–97).

"Do not be afraid of what you are about to suffer.... Be faithful, even to the point of death, and I will give you life as your victor's crown" (Revelation 2:10).

Evangelist again met up with the two travelers. They welcomed him and recited how their journey had progressed. Each pilgrim paid tribute to their friend, who had first set each on the way to salvation. During this present meeting Evangelist was called a prophet for he revealed something about their future. They *must go* through a certain town on the Way to the Celestial City, and it *will* involve suffering. Also, one of the pilgrims will experience a horrific death. Evangelist revealed that specific person in his prophecy: "Be faithful unto death."

Strangely enough, Bunyan cited the benefits of such a death: one pilgrim would enter heaven sooner and escape upcoming troubles. All this prepared the pilgrims for their next adventure at Vanity Fair, the town where they'd face much opposition as Christ-followers.

**My Takeaway:** We are not usually told about what's going to happen, and that's often best. If I knew that tomorrow I would be in a car wreck, I might not leave the house and miss the lessons that accident would teach me. If I knew the outcome of my family's financial future, I might make greedy decisions about our giving, and that would disrupt God's plan for us and those we could touch with the gospel. Foretelling the future is most often neither pleasant nor beneficial.

**Your Turn:** Are you satisfied not knowing what will happen in the future? Why or why not?

# Entering Vanity Fair
## WEEK FOUR DAY TWO

"One chanced mockingly, beholding the carriages of the men, to say unto them, *What will ye buy?* But they looking gravely upon him, said, *We buy the Truth*" (pp. 100–101).

"Buy the truth and do not sell it—wisdom, instruction and insight as well" (Proverbs 23:23).

Alexander Whyte, in his book *Bunyan Characters*, wrote: "Vanity Fair is one of John Bunyan's universally-admitted masterpieces" (p. 203). The fair's shopkeepers mocked the pilgrims even about their attire. But the crux of the harassment centered on the newcomers' outright rejection of the fair's trinkets: all vanity, worthless, and pleasure seeking. Since merchants rejected the truth and the pilgrims would not buy their vain wares, they trapped Christian and Faithful in a public cage. This sporting event humiliated the pilgrims, but they kept their resolve. As a result, a few from the town changed sides.

The townspeople indicted the pilgrims as "enemies and disturbers." They scheduled a trial with Judge Hate-Good presiding, and by that we know all was not going to fare well. True to their names, Christian and Faithful committed the outcome to Jesus who is fairest of all.

**My Takeaway:** For myself and those reading this book, it's rare that any of us has ever been sentenced to a physical trial about our testimony and good works. But I venture to say that some of us have experienced verbal ridicule and false accusations regarding our personal faith. When we are committed to speaking the truth and taking the consequences, it bears the image of Christ and His suffering. Voice of the Martyrs recounts present-day stories of the persecuted church worldwide. This faith-based organization is actively involved in upholding the faithful.

**Your Turn:** In what ways do you stand up for the truth and stay faithful to your testimony?

..................................................................................

..................................................................................

..................................................................................

..................................................................................

..................................................................................

..................................................................................

..................................................................................

..................................................................................

## Prosecutor's Witnesses
### WEEK FOUR DAY THREE

"My Lord, he doth, at once, not only condemn all our laudable doings, but us in the doing of them" (p. 105).

"But you—who are you to judge your neighbor?" (James 4:12). "Or do you not know that the Lord's people will judge the world?" (1 Corinthians 6:2).

The prosecutor called three witnesses to testify. Envy and Pickthank said they had known Faithful a long time, but Superstition had no acquaintance with him. All accusations stemmed from a judicial system opposed to goodness and fairness, for all was vanity in that town. Referring to their Prince, they meant Beelzebub (Satan) who had tempted Christ with his empty claim: "If you worship me, it will all be yours" (Luke 4:7). Of course, Christ did not buy into any of Satan's schemes. Christian and Faithful followed Christ's example.

Judge Hate-Good addressed the prisoner as "Renegade, Heretic, and Traitor," but called the witnesses "honest gentlemen." By this we know where the trial was headed, for their system was neither just nor according to righteous procedures. Truly, all was vanity, not fair.

**My Takeaway:** Like Christ, our citizenship is in heaven. Thus, we cannot be comfortable with this world's goods. The irony of the witnesses' statements lies in the fact that what they said was true and logical. Christianity and Vanity Fair "could not be reconciled"; their opposing customs would not please God. On a personal note: when our bank account was slim, my husband and I sought a remedy based on the wisdom of God. (See Romans 11:33.) Many a time God came through with His provision, not an overabundance but adequate and in a timely fashion.

**Your Turn:** Describe your search for what's good, just, righteous, and wise.

..................................................................................

..................................................................................

..................................................................................

..................................................................................

..................................................................................

..................................................................................

..................................................................................

..................................................................................

..................................................................................

# Faithful's Defense
## WEEK FOUR DAY FOUR

"In the worship of God there is required a Divine Faith; but there can be no Divine Faith without a Divine Revelation of the Will of God" (p. 107).

"I am put here for the defense of the gospel" (Philippians 1:16).

With some reluctance Judge Hate-Good gave Faithful a chance to speak in his defense. Faithful had something to say about each witness's statement. First, about Envy, he made a distinction between the custom of vain wares and those who sell them. Next, what Superstition said about pleasing God, Faithful pointed to divine revelation necessary to discern God's will. Lastly, about Pickthank's "honorable friends," such as Carnal-Delight, Luxurious, and Leachery, Faithful basically agreed with their names, making them fit for hell. Faithful closed his argument with "and so the Lord have mercy upon me."

Faithful spoke the truth, but that was not what the judge, witnesses, or townspeople wanted to hear. Evident that all were against him, this trial had no use for fair tactics. Yet Faithful remained true to God and his testimony. The truth held consequences for him.

**My Takeaway:** Of the two pilgrims, Faithful was the one on trial while Christian stood by. In video versions of *The Pilgrim's Progress* I saw Christian's dilemma, for he had no voice while his faithful companion faced an unfair trial. Being on trial is difficult, but standing by a friend on trial can be a heartbreaking experience. This has been the experience of Christian families in the persecuted areas of the world as they watch members beaten or killed. Yet they've stood true to the Lord and their faith. The persecuted church needs our prayers as well as our sympathy.

**Your Turn:** Play the role of either Faithful or Christian at the trial. Describe their position and response.

..............................................................................................
..............................................................................................
..............................................................................................
..............................................................................................
..............................................................................................
..............................................................................................
..............................................................................................

# Jury's Verdict

## WEEK FOUR DAY FIVE

"Then went the Jury out . . . who every one gave in his private verdict against him among themselves, and afterwards unanimously concluded to bring him in Guilty" (p. 108).

"But mark this: There will be terrible times in the last days. . . . In fact, everyone who wants to live a godly life in Christ Jesus will be persecuted" (2 Timothy 3:1, 12).

The judge addressed the jury whose names gave clues to their perceived verdict: Mr. Blind-man, the foreman, Mr. No-good, Mr. Malice, Mr. Love-lust, Mr. Live-loose, Mr. High-mind, Mr. Cruelty, and five others. Judge Hate-Good pointed out examples of their law based on the mandates of Pharaoh (Exodus 1), Nebuchadnezzar (Daniel 3), and Darius (Daniel 6). The jury also heard that this was an apparent crime, nothing much to deliberate.

As expected, the jury brought back a unanimous verdict of "Guilty." Each juror pronounced something offensive about the accused. For example, Mr. Malice said, "I hate the very looks of him," and Mr. Cruelty said, "Hanging is too good for him."

**My Takeaway:** Jesus warned His disciples, "If they persecuted me, they will persecute you also" (John 15:20), and He added, "They will treat you this way because of my name" (v. 21). The trial proved no surprise to Christian and Faithful; their names linked them to their persecution. Above that, they received cruel treatment because of their Savior's name. Their faithfulness connected them to their righteous Lord. History has proven the warning of Jesus true—during biblical times as well as the present-day persecuted church.

**Your Turn:** Find evidence of the persecuted church—past and present. What does this lead you to do?

..................................................................................................

..................................................................................................

..................................................................................................

..................................................................................................

..................................................................................................

..................................................................................................

..................................................................................................

..................................................................................................

..................................................................................................

# Transported

## WEEK FOUR DAY SIX

"Now I saw, that there stood behind the multitude a Chariot and a couple of horses waiting for *Faithful*, who . . . was taken up into it, and straitway was carried up through the clouds with Sound of Trumpet, the nearest way to the Celestial Gate" (p. 109).

"Suddenly a chariot of fire and horses of fire appeared . . . and Elijah went up to heaven in a whirlwind" (2 Kings 2:11).

Bunyan did not spare details of Faithful's "most cruel death." In accordance with the law of the town, the torture administered to any guilty party included scourging, lancing with knives, stoning, pricking with swords, and burning at the stake. The end of Faithful's life on earth suited his persecutors, but God was not finished with him. God provided an immediate escape with chariot and horses, accompanied by a trumpet sound, not unlike a celebration. Faithful's entrance into heaven was similar to the flight of Elijah.

After a short term again in prison, Christian escaped by the power of God's hand. As he continued his journey, Christian composed a song: "Sing, Faithful, sing, and let thy name survive; for though they killed thee, thou art yet alive" (p. 110).

**My Takeaway:** Faithful did not escape trial, guilty verdict, torture, or cruel death. He did remain faithful unto death as Evangelist had prophesied. We are not promised easy lives when we commit to follow Christ. Whatever the circumstances encountered in this life, we are promised life eternal. Our pledge is to remain faithful. God takes care of the rest.

**Your Turn:** What did you expect when you said yes to Christ? What has been your experience?

..........................................................................................

..........................................................................................

..........................................................................................

..........................................................................................

..........................................................................................

..........................................................................................

..........................................................................................

..........................................................................................

..........................................................................................

## Week Five: Good and Bad Company

# Hopeful Joined Christian
### WEEK FIVE DAY ONE

"Thus one died to make testimony to the Truth, and another rises out of his ashes to be a companion with Christian in his Pilgrimage" (p. 110).

"Epaphroditus, my brother, co-worker and fellow soldier . . . whom you sent to take care of my needs" (Philippians 2:25).

Hopeful, Christian's new companion, earned his name by watching Christian and Faithful in Vanity Fair. How they suffered became instrumental in Hopeful's pilgrimage. Hopeful reported that others from that wicked city would also follow later. The torture and death of Faithful advanced the gospel. Spoiler Alert: after many more trials and temptations, Christian and Hopeful will eventually enter the Celestial City together.

Throughout the book of Acts we learn about Paul's numerous traveling companions, notably

Luke who wrote the account. Reading this history of the early church, we notice the "we" passages, indicating where Luke accompanied Paul. Luke also cited other companions of Paul such as Barnabas, John Mark, Timothy, Gaius, and Aristarchus. Some of these helped establish what would later become Christian churches.

**My Takeaway:** It's encouraging to know we do not travel alone, for God has sent companions to enable us along life's journey. At the same time, He has asked us to comfort and aid others. Sometimes these fellow disciples are closer to us than our family members. My husband and I have mothers and fathers, sisters and brothers, in each church we've had the privilege to serve.

**Your Turn:** Give an account about a valued companion on your Christian walk. Or tell how you have been an encourager for another Christian.

..............................................................................................

..............................................................................................

..............................................................................................

..............................................................................................

..............................................................................................

..............................................................................................

..............................................................................................

..............................................................................................

# Rich Friends in Fair-speech
## WEEK FIVE DAY TWO

"*Christian:* This town of Fair-speech . . . they say it's a wealthy place. *By-ends:* Yes, I will assure you that it is, and I have very many rich kindred there" (p. 111).

"The rich have many friends" (Proverbs 14:20). "Command them to do good, to be rich in good deeds, and to be generous and willing to share" (1 Timothy 6:18).

A new traveler from Fair-speech was proud of his friends: Turn-about, Time-server, Lord Fair-speech (for whom the town was named), also Mr. Smooth-man, Facing-both-ways, Any-thing, and the parson Two-tongues. Their names revealed their character, and their riches did not connect with good deeds. Christian knew of this town, and he asked the traveler his name. By-ends did not own up to his name, saying it was put upon him in a malicious manner.

Bunyan gave the clue as to the *ends by* which this man lived. By-ends and the two pilgrims parted company, for he would not own religion in rags but only with "silver slippers." We learn more about By-ends from three travelers who joined him later: Mr. Hold-the-World, Mr. Money-love, and Mr. Save-all, all taught by Mr. Gripe-man.

**My Takeaway:** Reading about all these rich folks, I see clearly the contrast in Jesus who left heaven and became poor for us, that we "through his poverty might become rich" (2 Corinthians 8:9; Philippians 2:6–11). With this should be the admonition to look to ourselves. By what ends do I strive? Do I find my motivation in the world's goods, or do I seek the standard Jesus left me to follow? The Westminster Shorter Catechism advises: "Glorify God and enjoy Him forever."

**Your Turn:** In your actions, what is your intended end? In other words, what is the goal of your Christian walk?

..............................................................................................

..............................................................................................

..............................................................................................

..............................................................................................

..............................................................................................

..............................................................................................

..............................................................................................

..............................................................................................

# What Gain for What Reason?

## WEEK FIVE DAY THREE

A "good wife, and good customers, and good gain, and all these by becoming religious, which is good: Therefore, to become religious . . . is a good and profitable design" (p. 117).

"Judas Iscariot—went to the chief priests and asked, 'What are you willing to give me if I deliver him over to you?' So they counted out for him thirty pieces of silver" (Matthew 26:14–15).

By-ends posed a question to his friends: By what means can a zealous man obtain religion? Mr. Money-love gave an answer with four parts: putting conscience aside, considering whatever makes a man better, applying his temper to the task, and exchanging a small gain for a great end. He concluded that even gaining a rich wife would be virtuous for the cause of religion. Friends gave examples of good men who were also rich—Abraham, Solomon, and Job—asserting that both Scripture and reason sided with their argument.

Since Christian and Hopeful were still within sight, this group decided to pose the same question to them, especially since they had opposed Mr. By-ends. Christian answered their question with examples of those who enjoyed the world above Christ. Hypocrites gave a pretense with long prayers; Judas gained a bag of coins but lost his life; and Simon, a sorcerer, became a believer but offered money to receive the Holy Spirit for the power he could gain.

**My Takeaway:** To follow Christ only to have our natural desires satisfied is wrong. Though Jesus fed the crowds, he also rebuked them. "Do not work for food that spoils, but for food that endures to eternal life" (John 6:27). In our churches today we often emphasize more the how of worship than Whom we worship. Eternity is to be valued over personal preferences.

**Your Turn:** How do you respond to these words of a worship song: "So forget about yourself and concentrate on Him and worship Him"?

..................................................................................

..................................................................................

..................................................................................

..................................................................................

..................................................................................

# Come and See

## WEEK FIVE DAY FOUR

"A little off the road, over against the Silver-Mine, stood Demas (gentleman-like) to call to passengers to come and see . . . Then said Hopeful, Let us go see" (p. 120).

"Do your best to come to me quickly, for Demas, because he loved this world, has deserted me and has gone to Thessalonica" (2 Timothy 4:9–10).

For a brief but pleasant time Christian and Hopeful visited a narrow plain called Ease. At the far end, a Silver-Mine lay hidden in a little hill called Lucre. Guarding this treasure, Demas bid the pilgrims "come and see." Curious, Hopeful wanted to investigate; for Demas's description sounded inviting. Christian, however, had heard about this place and its trap, luring seekers even to their death.

Thus Christian questioned Demas about his name and heritage, calling him an enemy of the King. Christian was more concerned about giving a good account to his Lord, fearing shame and desiring boldness when he would stand before the Judge of all peoples.

The pilgrims speculated how By-ends would respond when he came to this place. Sure enough By-ends and his friends fell prey to the temptation and they "never were seen again."

**My Takeaway:** "Come and see" reminds me of how my husband's preacher-uncle summed up the path to sin in three words: Look. Desire. Take. Among others are two biblical examples: Eve and David. Eve saw the fruit as pleasant, then she desired and took it, ignoring what God had told her. David looked across to another roof, desired Bathsheba, and took her for his own.

**Your Turn:** Apply those same words "come and see" to some temptation into which you have fallen. If you need forgiveness, ask our loving Father God.

# Remember Lot's Wife
## WEEK FIVE DAY FIVE

"They both concluded that that was the Pillar of Salt into which Lot's wife was turned" (p. 123).

"No one in the field should go back for anything. Remember Lot's wife! Whoever tries to keep their life will lose it, and whoever loses their life will preserve it" (Luke 17:31–33).

The pilgrims came upon a monument and at first had some difficulty determining what it represented. Christian, the more learned of the two, read a sign posted at the top: "Remember Lot's Wife." They did just that, considering one who disobeyed and looked back because of her "covetous heart" (p. 123). Strategically placed, the monument served as an example of what might have happened to them had they accepted Demas's invitation to see the silver mine.

Hopeful admitted his foolish desire and said, "Let grace be adored, and let me be ashamed." Note the imagery here: grace adored (loved and praised) and man ashamed—as Lot's wife escaped one peril (Sodom's destruction) to fall by her own desire.

The next scene served as a contrast when the pilgrims came upon a river, called the Water of Life by the apostle John. The water refreshed them. The leaves from nearby fruit trees held medicinal quality. Here they found safety and gathered fruit for their journey.

**My Takeaway:** In Sodom two angels grabbed the hands of Lot, his wife, and their two daughters, and commanded, "Flee for your lives! Don't look back" (Genesis 19:17). Lot's wife did not step out of the prescribed way, but she did look back. With one act of disobedience, Lot's wife determined her fate. Total obedience and surrender to God's will is the only way to live.

**Your Turn:** The mighty arm of God is stretched out for our deliverance and defense. Cite one incident in which God has defended you.

...........................................................................................

...........................................................................................

...........................................................................................

...........................................................................................

...........................................................................................

...........................................................................................

...........................................................................................

...........................................................................................

# The Way Back
## WEEK FIVE DAY SIX

Christian said, "Here is the easiest going; come, good Hopeful, and let us go over" (p. 126). "The Way of going back was very dangerous" (p. 128).

"Set up road signs; put up guideposts. Take note of the highway, the road that you take. Return." (Jeremiah 31:21).

Keeping on the Way, the pilgrims soon found the road rough to their tender feet. Discouragement set in. On the other side of a fence a meadow looked appealing and easier to travel. Christian did not hesitate to cross over and enjoy the easy path. Walking in By-path Meadow, they briefly saw a man named Vain-Confidence who assured them they would reach the Celestial City that way. Soon darkness overtook them and they doubted their decision.

Christian asked forgiveness from Hopeful for leading them astray. Now it was time to go back and find the true Way. Hopeful decided to lead, for Christian's mind might be troubled. The river waters rose and proved to be dangerous. Finding a little shelter, they rested and soon slept.

**My Takeaway:** Looking for an easier path, one finds the way back is often long and hard. Before Joshua died, he gave the Israelites a choice—to follow God or their own gods. He reminded them that God is holy and jealous, and He might not forgive if they persisted in their own way. (Find the account in Joshua, chapters 23 and 24.) A choice to serve God and Him alone does not promise a rose-strewn path, but He will be with us throughout our whole journey. The promise of His presence is worth the hard knots along the Way. Amen.

**Your Turn:** How do you relate to the following verse? "Watch and pray so that you will not fall into temptation. The spirit is willing, but the flesh is weak" (Matthew 26:41).

## Week Six: Doubt Led to Despair

# Doubting Castle
### WEEK SIX DAY ONE

"Now there was, not far from the place where they lay, a castle, called Doubting Castle, the owner whereof was Giant Despair, and it was in his grounds they now were sleeping" (p. 128).

"When you ask, you must believe and not doubt, because the one who doubts is like a wave of the sea, blown and tossed by the wind" (James 1:6).

Giant Despair caught the pilgrims sleeping, and he accused them of trespassing on his grounds. Asking why they were there, the giant heard that Christian and Hopeful had lost their way. Thus he forced them to go to his castle, leading them to a dark dungeon, "nasty and stinking." Being in the castle's prison threw the pilgrims in doubt, for they had to admit they were at fault. Their hasty decision to avoid the right Way, they went an easier way. They landed in prison, guarded now by a despicable giant. For four days they had no food or drink, not even light. They also suffered beatings from the giant, but the worst was how the pilgrims wrestled with their doubts.

**My Takeaway:** While it is no sin to have some doubts, questioning our faith and its foundations, this season might bring with it unstable thought patterns. James, leader of the early New Testament church, cautioned his readers that doubt can toss believers around like waves of the sea. Doubt can be good when it moves us to find answers that firm up our faith. Seeking the truth through God's Word is the pathway to a firm foundation for individuals and the church.

**Your Turn:** What doubts have haunted you in your walk of faith and how did you find answers? What resources did you use: Scripture and/or mentors in the church?

..........................................................................................

..........................................................................................

..........................................................................................

..........................................................................................

..........................................................................................

..........................................................................................

..........................................................................................

..........................................................................................

# Giant Despair and His Wife
## WEEK SIX DAY TWO

The giant "withdraws, and leaves them there to condole their misery, and to mourn under their distress" (p. 130).

"You have put me in the lowest pit, in the darkest depths. Your wrath lies heavily on me.... I am confined and cannot escape" (Psalm 88:6, 7, 8).

Giant Despair. No wonder he was a giant, for despair can surely blow life's problems out of proportion. In this dark and nasty dungeon, Christian and Hopeful got bogged down with distress and trouble. They only had each other, and felt they could turn nowhere else.

Giant Despair had a wife named Diffidence, defined as distrust because of lack of confidence. However, this dictionary finding doesn't seem to fit her. She advised her husband to beat the prisoners without mercy. The first morning he berated them verbally "as if they were dogs" (p. 130); then he used a crab-tree limb to beat them. The harsh treatment by Despair and Diffidence was meant to persuade the prisoners to take their own lives.

This idea appealed to Christian. Using Scripture, Hopeful latched onto hope and reasoned with his friend. The giant's wife, Diffidence, concluded rightly that the prisoners lived in hope (p. 133).

**My Takeaway:** One night, years ago, my husband and I knelt by our bed and asked God for His guidance, an assurance of hope. With the door of one job closed, we did not see even an open window for a new course. Within a week the answer came—an invitation literally to walk across the street to a new position. During that week of waiting on God, we had only to trust Him.

**Your Turn:** Perhaps in your life a door closed and nothing looked promising. How did you handle that and what answer did God send in His timing?

..................................................................................

..................................................................................

..................................................................................

..................................................................................

..................................................................................

..................................................................................

..................................................................................

..................................................................................

..................................................................................

..................................................................................

# What Shall We Do?
## WEEK SIX DAY THREE

Christian said, "The Grave is more easy for me than this Dungeon! Shall we be ruled by the Giant?" (pp. 130–131).

"I prefer strangling and death, rather than this body of mine. I despise my life; I would not live forever. Let me alone; my days have no meaning" (Job 7:15, 16).

Once again Christian said, "What shall we do?" (p. 130) The first time he asked this, he had read the Book and became convicted of his sin. Evangelist arrived to help him. Now in the dungeon, the two pilgrims had no helper. Or, did they? I cite an incident from Scripture:

Elisha the prophet warned the king of Israel that the Arameans had positioned themselves for war. Early one morning Elisha's servant saw the enemy's horses and chariots surrounding the city. He asked, "What shall we do?" Elisha told him not to be afraid; then he prayed, "Lord, open my servant's eyes." With new vision, he saw the hills full of horses and chariots of fire. The Lord struck the enemy with blindness, and they stopped raiding Israel. (2 Kings 6:8–23.)

**My Takeaway:** Too often I've felt alone, even hopeless, as if God had withdrawn His help. I've cried out to God for fear of what might happen next. Restored, I came to believe that all the while God upheld me with His strong and steady hand. Help *was* on the way. God is always present, never leaving us to work on our own. "And we know that in all things God works for the good of those who love him" (Romans 8:28).

**Your Turn:** Recall a time when you thought nothing good could come out of your circumstance. Then remember how God did work things out for your good. Praise Him.

.................................................................................

.................................................................................

.................................................................................

.................................................................................

.................................................................................

.................................................................................

.................................................................................

.................................................................................

.................................................................................

.................................................................................

# Hopeful Lived Up to His Name

## WEEK SIX DAY FOUR

"For one to kill himself is to kill Body and Soul at once.... All the Law is not in the hand of Giant Despair.... Let's be patient, and endure a while" (p. 131).

"Those who hope in the Lord will renew their strength" (Isaiah 40:31). "My times are in your hands; deliver me from the hands of my enemies" (Psalm 31:15).

Being ruled by the giant not only meant the pilgrims received punishment at his hand, but the giant also counseled them to make an end of their lives. Christian was almost persuaded thus, but Hopeful chose to look for counsel in God's word. Admitting that their "present condition was dreadful" (p. 131), Hopeful asserted that suicide would be to destroy not only their bodies but their souls as well. We conclude that someone who commits suicide would have no time for repentance. Would this mean no hope for eternal life? We leave the answer to such questions in the hands of our sovereign God, for we are not qualified to decide matters of judgment.

Our biblical example would be the life of Job, who suffered much at the hands of Satan and without cause or explanation. Even Job's wife said, "Curse God and die!" (Job 2:9). His friends offered no good counsel. After a long wait God met Job, but he received no satisfactory explanation for his suffering. God's questions drove Job to admit that God is sovereign.

**My Takeaway:** Years ago my husband experienced endogenous depression. While one usual symptom is suicidal thoughts, we are thankful that never entered his mind. Plagued with disillusionment, he doubted his abilities to do what God called him to do. With God's healing, along with medication and psychiatric help, he recovered, but with lingering side effects.

**Your Turn:** Have you ever been to the point of despair, and if so, how did you cope with it?

...........................................................................................
...........................................................................................
...........................................................................................
...........................................................................................
...........................................................................................
...........................................................................................

# Remember Past Victories
## WEEK SIX DAY FIVE

"My Brother, said Hopeful, remembrest thou not . . . what hardship, terror, and amazement hast thou already gone through, and art thou now nothing but fear?" (p. 132).

"To him who led his people through the wilderness; *His love endures forever*. . . . and freed us from our enemies. *His love endures forever*" (Psalm 136:16, 24).

Christian was still not convinced their dreadful state could be better than death. Hopeful took another tactic: he recited Christian's past victories. He had been through the Valley of the Shadow of Death, defeated Apollyon in a fierce battle, and stood true to his convictions during many hardships along the Way. Hopeful laid his own life alongside his companion, reminding Christian that he "played the man at Vanity Fair, and was neither afraid of the chain nor cage" (pp. 132–133). Hopeful pointed Christian to avoid shame and redirect his thoughts.

The scene shifted to Giant Despair and Diffidence as they lay in bed. The giant reported that the prisoners had not taken his advice to "make away themselves" (p. 133). So he planned a tour the next day: to visit the bones of earlier prisoners and to threaten the pilgrims that he would soon tear them in pieces. This also failed to persuade the two pilgrims.

**My Takeaway:** Throughout the Old Testament, the Lord instructed the Israelites to rehearse their pilgrimage and the protection He provided. In David's psalms he gave credence to the Lord's deliverance of His people. Psalm 136 is one example of that rehearsal, with repetition of the phrase "His love endures forever" after each remembrance of the Lord's unfailing love.

**Your Turn:** Recite from your spiritual history some victory that moved you from a season of doubt and defeat to a glorious time of renewal and restoration.

.......................................................................................
.......................................................................................
.......................................................................................
.......................................................................................
.......................................................................................
.......................................................................................
.......................................................................................

# Key of Promise

## WEEK SIX DAY SIX

"I have a key in my bosom, called Promise, that will I am persuaded open any lock in Doubting Castle [said Christian]. Then said Hopeful, That's good news . . . pluck it out . . . and try" (p. 134).

"You make known to me the path of life; you will fill me with joy in your presence, with eternal pleasures at your right hand" (Psalm 16:11).

About midnight Christian and Hopeful began to pray and continued to pray until daybreak. Blinded by his circumstances and quite surprised at his forgetfulness, Christian suddenly remembered he had a key called Promise. Inserted into the lock of the dungeon, the door easily flew open. Two more doors yielded to the key and the pilgrims walked away. But the creaking of the lock in the gate awakened the giant who thus pursued them.

However, the light of day did its work on the giant whose limbs failed him. This hindered him sorely and he succumbed to fits of weakness. His passion for punishment could only be performed in the dark. We need to remember this lesson:

"People loved darkness instead of light because their deeds were evil" (John 3:19). In contrast, the two pilgrims could "declare the praises of him who called [them] out of darkness into his wonderful light" (1 Peter 2:9).

**My Takeaway:** Alexander Whyte, in his book *Bunyan Characters,* pointed out that Bunyan in his own story had several promise keys. Among them: "Return unto me, for I have redeemed you" (Isaiah 44:22) and "My grace is sufficient for you" (2 Corinthians 12:9). When my husband was in the hospital for 24 days, I found a fitting promise key—"Taste and see that the Lord is good" (Psalm 34:8). That led me out of darkness into God's glorious light.

**Your Turn:** Gather a ring of promise keys from your life and cite a few here:

.................................................................................

.................................................................................

.................................................................................

.................................................................................

.................................................................................

.................................................................................

.................................................................................

.................................................................................

## Week Seven: Beware of Shortcuts

# Escaped and Refreshed
## WEEK SEVEN DAY ONE

"They went then till they came to the Delectable Mountains . . . where also they drank and washed themselves" (p. 135).

"He has given us his very great and precious promises . . . having escaped the corruption in the world caused by evil desires" (2 Peter 1:4).

Back on the King's Highway, the two pilgrims erected a pillar to warn other travelers of the dangers of Doubting Castle and Giant Despair. At the Delectable Mountains they came to a garden with fruit and fountains of water. They had escaped further punishment by Giant Despair, but they had yet to be restored from the beatings and verbal assaults. The pilgrims needed refreshment for their spirits along with healing for their wounds. The vineyards provided means for both physical and spiritual health.

The water offered both inner and outer refreshing while it quenched thirst and washed their bodies. Provisions of food, drink, and cleansing came freely to Christian and Hopeful. And to whom did these gifts belong? To the Lord of the Hill, and rightly so. "Every good and perfect gift is from above, coming down from the Father" (James 1:17).

**My Takeaway:** Too often we neglect time for renewal after intense stress or physical adversity. Even hospitals release patients too quickly. "Get Well Quick" is a repeated sentiment, but it's not realistic. Proper healing takes time to be restored to full health, physically, emotionally, and spiritually. Returning home after delivery of each child, I took time off from duties outside the home, accepted help from family and friends, and concentrated on renewal of body and spirit.

**Your Turn:** Have you taken time for renewal when needed? What was the cause and how did you manage?

..........................................................................................
..........................................................................................
..........................................................................................
..........................................................................................
..........................................................................................
..........................................................................................

# Within Sight of the City
## WEEK SEVEN DAY TWO

"These mountains are Emmanuel's Land, and they are within sight of his City; and the sheep also are his, and he laid down his life for them" (p. 136).

"'I am the good shepherd. The good shepherd lays down his life for the sheep'" (John 10:11).

On the mountain range Christian and Hopeful met four shepherds whose names were Knowledge, Experience, Watchful, and Sincere. Their first encounter seemed to be spoken in riddles, with the pilgrims asking questions and the shepherds answering. Is this the Way? You are in the Way. How far to the Celestial City? Too far for some, but not for those who continue. Is the Way safe or dangerous? Safe for those who desire it; but transgressors will fall away. Is there a place for relief? We do not forget to entertain strangers. (p. 136)

Then the conversation shifted to questions the pilgrims usually encountered: From where did you come and how have you persevered along the

Way? Their answers opened up the opportunity for them to stay and rest during the night.

**My Takeaway:** "The sheep also are his" (p. 136) reminds me of a story I'd heard about the evangelist Billy Sunday (1862–1935), former outfielder for the Chicago White Stockings. He quoted Psalm 50:10. The Lord said "every animal of the forest is mine, and the cattle on a thousand hills." To this Sunday added, "and the taters under those hills" (my paraphrase). While this gives us assurance that God supplies our needs, it mainly indicates that God doesn't need anything. He owns everything. The pilgrims found that out, and we can also live out that truth.

**Your Turn:** Have you taken advantage of God's abundant supply? How?

# Shepherds Lead

## WEEK SEVEN DAY THREE

"Then said the Shepherds . . . Shall we show these Pilgrims some Wonders?" (p. 137).

"Do your best to present yourself to God as one approved, a worker who does not need to be ashamed and who correctly handles the word of truth" (2 Timothy 2:15).

The four Shepherds were unified in purpose; their names represented attributes of a pastor. A servant of the Master must seek and obtain Knowledge for leading the people. Experience is necessary, having a background of training and a personal relationship with Christ. A minister has to be Watchful for snares of his own doing but also recognize temptations among the flock. A pastor's work includes a Sincere personal life reflecting the character of Christ.

The Shepherds led Hopeful and Christian to places with spiritual meanings. First, they saw a steep hill called Error. Travelers lay below, dashed and unburied, as examples of those who fell from the true Way. Looking past a mountain named Caution, they saw among the tombs blind men who had stumbled. Christian and Hopeful wept. Their own predicament had come about because they chose an easier way and ended up in Doubting Castle.

**My Takeaway:** Shepherds are trained to lead their flock to safety. Sheep need tending; they are often careless about their needs and unable to stay on the way. With his staff, a shepherd will rescue a wandering lamb and get him back on the right path. One specific time in our marriage, my husband heeded God's call to stay on course: "This is the way; walk in it" (Isaiah 30:21). It made the difference between quitting and finishing school. Our Good Shepherd was Watchful.

**Your Turn:** Apply the four Shepherds' names to times when you needed any of their qualities.

...........................................................................................
...........................................................................................
...........................................................................................
...........................................................................................
...........................................................................................
...........................................................................................
...........................................................................................
...........................................................................................
...........................................................................................

# The Way of Understanding
## WEEK SEVEN DAY FOUR

"He that wandereth out of the Way of Understanding shall remain in the Congregation of the Dead" (p. 138).

"Folly brings joy to one who has no sense, but whoever has understanding keeps a straight course" (Proverbs 15:21).

The Shepherds described what had become of those who chose the wrong way. Perhaps they had seen Christian and Hopeful as they deserted the way and followed an easier path, ending up at Doubting Castle? But the pilgrims had escaped and did not suffer death at the hands of Giant Despair. They felt shame and sorrow, but did not express this to the Shepherds.

Opening a door in the side of a hill, the Shepherds bid the pilgrims look in. What they saw and heard was foreboding: dark and smoky, along with "a rumbling noise, as of fire" (p. 139). This revealed a "by-way to Hell" where could be found such hypocrites as Esau who sold his birthright (Genesis 25), Judas who betrayed his Master (Matthew 26), and

Ananias and Sapphira who lied and deceived the apostles (Acts 5).

Hopeful observed that all these persons had at one time started their pilgrimage to the Celestial City, yet turned away. The pilgrims resolved to plead for strength needed during the rest of their journey. The Shepherds agreed they would require such strength.

**My Takeaway:** Sad that a friend had left his wife for another woman, I wondered how he could forsake his vows. Although totally unrelated, I thought of some of my own weaknesses. Along life's way I've required strength to stay consistent in following God's plan for me.

**Your Turn:** Read about the narrow way in Luke 13:22–30. Then pray for family and friends who are on the broad way.

# Clear Perspective
## WEEK SEVEN DAY FIVE

"Let us here show to the Pilgrims the Gates of the Celestial City, if they have skill to look through our Perspective-Glass" (p. 139).

"Remember those earlier days after you had received the light, when you endured in a great conflict full of suffering" (Hebrews 10:32).

Before the Pilgrims set out again on their journey, the Shepherds desired to show them the Gates of the Celestial City through their unique Perspective-Glass. It was more than a telescopic looking glass; it added perspective to their view. The Shepherds led them to the top of a high hill appropriately called Clear.

Their past experience of wrongdoing and what they had seen of the by-way to Hell at first marred their perspective of the beautiful Gate. Those remembrances instilled guilt over their past and even made their hands shake as they held the looking glass. Then after seeing the glory of the City, they sang about "things deep, things hid," and mysterious (p. 140).

God himself provides the beautiful and true light of Heaven. The tabernacle in the wilderness and Solomon's temple in Jerusalem both shown with the glory of God's presence. In this life we can see a bit of God's glory; in Heaven we shall behold His glory.

**My Takeaway:** God uses our memory to remind us of the past so we do not repeat our sins. At the same time, He wants us to see clearly His love, mercy, and grace in the examples of what Jesus has done. These bring perspective to our relationship and give hope for our future.

**Your Turn:** Light represents truth for living in the world today. Jesus sheds enough light for our paths. Tell how you depend on His light daily.

# Secrets and Warnings
## WEEK SEVEN DAY SIX

"*Take Heed that they sleep not upon the Inchanted Ground*" (p. 140).

"Keep watch because you do not know when the owner of the house will come back. . . . If he comes suddenly, do not let him find you sleeping" (Mark 13:35, 36).

The Pilgrims sang of secrets revealed to them by the Shepherds, kept concealed from others in a mysterious fashion. While rejoicing over their visit, they prepared to leave but not without some warnings from their hosts. Each of the four Shepherds spoke their farewell: the first gave them a note for the Way, perhaps to read later. The second warned, "Beware of the Flatterer," for they would meet him soon. The third also gave warning not to sleep upon the Enchanted Ground. The fourth bid them "God speed." Were they then ready to continue their journey to the Celestial City? We'll soon find out. But first . . .

Bunyan interjected, "I awoke from my dream" (p. 140). Scholars have suggested that this may have related to Bunyan's release from prison. Although his time in prison was interrupted, he had to return there. It's also possible this referred to Bunyan's victory over despair.

Bunyan slept and dreamed again, seeing Christian and Hopeful on their way down the mountains toward the Celestial City. First, they traveled on a crooked lane through the country of Conceit. Ahead they met some interesting but mostly unsavory characters.

**My Takeaway:** Friends gave advice when I prepared for mission trips, for they had traveled to those places ahead of me. They provided tips for what to pack, some even gave me notes to bring to those we'd see. They also warned about how to act and what to wear. I needed their advice.

**Your Turn:** What important secrets (or even warnings) have been entrusted to you?

..................................................................................

..................................................................................

..................................................................................

..................................................................................

..................................................................................

..................................................................................

..................................................................................

## Week Eight: Snared by Flattery

# Ignorance Added Nothing
## WEEK EIGHT DAY ONE

"When Christian saw that the man was wise in his own conceit, he said to Hopeful whisperingly, *There is more hopes of a Fool than of him*" (p. 141).

"For it is God's will that by doing good you should silence the ignorant talk of foolish people" (1 Peter 2:15).

Along the crooked path, the Pilgrims met a native of the country of Conceit named Ignorance. Even though he traveled toward the Celestial City, he had no certificate. He assumed his good deeds were enough for entrance. Christian pointed out there is no other way than by the Cross. Content to follow his own way, Ignorance proved he was a fool. The pilgrims debated whether they could offer any good advice for him. Hopeful stated that no further discourse should be given. The two moved on ahead while Ignorance followed.

# Ignorance Added Nothing | 95

Later in their travels, the pilgrims invited Ignorance to walk with them. Hopeful asked about his soul and Christian asked what gave him comfort. While their talk advanced to examination of one's heart, Ignorance tried to convince them of his good heart. He pointed out his faith did rest on obedience to duty, not on Christ's righteous death for sin. Thus he decided to travel alone. Christian stated then that Ignorance waxed "presumptuously confident" (p. 174).

**My Takeaway:** According to the law, ignorance is no excuse. We don't break the law; the law breaks us. Apply this to civil law and God's Law. I found this to be true as a child, trying to skirt firm rules my parents made. Every time, their rules found me broken over my wrongdoing.

**Your Turn:** Have you used ignorance for an excuse after being caught in a wrong? How did that turn out for you?

......................................................................................
......................................................................................
......................................................................................
......................................................................................
......................................................................................
......................................................................................
......................................................................................

# Little-Faith

## WEEK EIGHT DAY TWO

"As for a great heart, Little-Faith had none" (p. 147).

"The disciples came to Jesus in private and asked, 'Why couldn't we drive it [a demon] out?' He replied, 'Because you have so little faith'" (Matthew 17:19, 20a).

Hopeful and Christian came upon a man bound with seven strong cords. At first they thought he was Turn-away, but then recognized him as Little-Faith. Christian told his friend about this fellow who had been robbed by Faint-heart, Mistrust, and Guilt. They had taken his money purse but not his Jewels (his certificate of saving faith). Not using faith wisely, he complained often about his state of affairs, allowing the thieves to take away his joy.

Hopeful compared Little-Faith with Esau who sold his birthright. Christian disagreed with his companion. He cited Peter who failed when confronted by the enemy, also Moses and David, proud men who fell but later humbled themselves under God's mighty hand (1 Peter 5:6).

Jesus found "little faith" in His disciples when they failed to cast out a demon (Matthew 17:16). Then Jesus explained that even faith as tiny as a mustard seed had the ability to move mountains (v. 20). It seemed a matter of focusing faith on God who does the impossible.

**My Takeaway:** During a rough time at one church, we trusted God with the matter. Besides, it was not in our hands to make a decision. God had given protection through past troubles, so we held onto His promise of hope for the future. As we waited, God's timing proved true. "For it is God who works in you to will and to act in order to fulfill his good purpose" (Philippians 2:13).

**Your Turn:** When and how has your little faith grown to trust God more fully for victory?

# Great-Grace

## WEEK EIGHT DAY THREE

"True, they have often fled, both they and their Master, when Great-Grace hath but appeared; and no marvel, for he is the King's Champion" (p. 148).

"Goliath stood and shouted to the ranks of Israel, 'Why do you come out and line up for battle? . . . Choose a man and have him come down to me.'" (1 Samuel 17:8).

Christian told of the King's champion, Great-Grace, who frightened away the three tormentors—Faint-heart, Mistrust, and Guilt—and even their master Satan. Defensive wounds marked Great-Grace's face, for we learn that he had "despaired even of life" (p. 149). Christian admitted that even with a coat of armor, his own battle with Apollyon left him wounded.

As a youth, David would qualify as the King's champion when he slew the giant Goliath. Peter, while he had a slow start, became a giant among the early church leaders. Throughout church history many Christian soldiers fought stiff battles with the enemy, verbally and physically. Among those martyrs were Stephen, the apostle Paul, Hugh Latimer, Thomas Becket, and Dietrich Bonhoeffer, to name a few. Showing great grace, these faithful warriors could recite with David, "You, Lord, have helped me and comforted me" (Psalm 86:17).

**My Takeaway:** When someone points out my faults or failures, I get defensive and that doesn't win the favor of others. Mistrust leads the way, followed by guilt. If I were in the right, I would not have to strike a defensive blow. Instead, what I need during these personal battles is to trust my true Defender and His faithfulness. It would also help to know the other's point of view.

**Your Turn:** How about you? How do you handle it when someone points out your faults?

# Flatterers

## WEEK EIGHT DAY FOUR

"Now do I see myself in error. Did not the Shepherds bid us beware of the Flatterers?" (p. 152).

"Those who flatter their neighbors are spreading nets for their feet" (Proverbs 29:5).

Once again the Way did not seem clearly marked. "They saw a way put itself into *their Way*" (p. 152). Two parallel paths appeared straight, so the pilgrims pondered which one to take. While they considered their choice, a stranger came alongside. Robed in light, he bid them follow him. By small increments the path turned them away from the true Way.

The stranger spun a net around the pilgrims. Trapped! Ashamed! They cried about their foolishness. They had not looked at the map, and thus followed a flatterer. Suddenly the man, disguised as an angel of light, left. Sent by the true Prince, a Shining One arrived, questioned them, and cut the net. However, he carried a whip and punished them so they would remember their foolish behavior.

They repented, received forgiveness, thanked their deliverer, and sang.

The Shining One told the pilgrims to heed what the Shepherds had given them: a map and warnings. Back on the Way, the pilgrims met a man walking toward them. Atheist was his name, not surprising, for he said that a king and kingdom did not exist. He tried to persuade them to turn around. This flatterer's advice they did not heed, choosing to walk by faith to the City.

**My Takeaway:** A friend told me that he doesn't have a bad memory; he just has a good forgetter. His humor reminds me that spiritual forgetfulness can get me into trouble. In C.S. Lewis's book, *The Silver Chair*, Aslan instructed Jill Pole to repeat his signs over and over during their journey. This theme of rehearsal is to our advantage and found often in the Bible.

**Your Turn:** What Bible verses remind you of God's faithfulness or warnings of danger ahead?

..............................................................................................

..............................................................................................

..............................................................................................

..............................................................................................

..............................................................................................

..............................................................................................

# Hopeful's Testimony
## WEEK EIGHT DAY FIVE

"That without the Righteousness of this Christ, all the World could not save me" (p. 163).

"I pray that the eyes of your heart may be enlightened in order that you may know the hope to which he has called you" (Ephesians 1:18a).

Entering the Enchanted Ground, Hopeful felt sleepy, but Christian came up with a plan to avoid what the Shepherds had warned them about that place. Thus a good discussion kept their minds alert. Hopeful recited his decision to take the journey, and it turned out to be a long process. He confessed to the enjoyment of sin, participating in behaviors abundant in Vanity Fair. Conviction of wrongdoing seesawed with performing religious duties, all to no good end.

Hopeful could not easily rid himself of sin and guilt. Faithful helped him focus on Christ, to come to that place of revelation. With a Bible that Faithful gave Hopeful, he searched for what God said about his condition. Told to pray, he did this over and over, but without any assurance of salvation. At last

Hopeful found the missing piece—Christ, the sure Word of God. When Hopeful looked upon Jesus, he saw his own sinfulness and Christ's righteousness. He accepted the salvation based only on Christ's sacrificial death—for past and present sins. Hopeful stated he loved all people; thus he was open for fellowship with Jesus and others.

**My Takeaway:** Each of us has a unique, personal testimony. Our paths of resistance and submission are different. Christian and Hopeful testified about how God brought them into the Way; each story differed in timing and nature. My testimony is not yours; yours is not mine.

**Your Turn:** Sum up your story. Write your Christian testimony, limited by space provided here.

...........................................................................................................

...........................................................................................................

...........................................................................................................

...........................................................................................................

...........................................................................................................

...........................................................................................................

...........................................................................................................

...........................................................................................................

...........................................................................................................

...........................................................................................................

# Good Use of Fear

## WEEK EIGHT DAY SIX

"Fear tends much to men's good, and to make them right at their beginning to go on Pilgrimage" (p. 173).

"The fear of the Lord is the beginning of knowledge" (Proverbs 1:7).

Continuing their discourse in the Enchanted Ground, the pilgrims talked some more about Ignorance, then moved on to examine people who lived in the City of Destruction. Bunyan used this practice of the Puritans to inject talk along practical yet doctrinal lines. Remembering such men as Temporary and Turnback who lived in Graceless, the conversation naturally turned to the subject of backsliding. This term, common in the Old Testament, was meant to label those who gave a verbal testimony but did not show change of heart and lifestyle.

Hopeful cited examples of a backslidden condition: mindful of one's conscience but not changed; fearful of what people thought but not of God's judgment; and shameful but still prideful.

Christian added the manner in which people backslide: forgetting the judgment to come; gradually leaving off private devotions; shunning the company of good Christians and public duty; and gossiping about believers, they return to former associates. They secretly yearn for carnal ways and "begin to play with little sins openly" (p. 178), showing their true selves.

**My Takeaway:** Fear can be good, the kind of fear that means respect, preventing us from doing wrong. John Newton wrote about that fear in his beloved song, "Amazing Grace." "'Twas grace that taught my heart to fear, And grace my fears relieved." I am grateful for a conscience that teaches me to fear/respect God, and then His grace eradicates any fear of His wrath.

**Your Turn:** How would you explain to someone that fear can be a good thing?

.........................................................................................
.........................................................................................
.........................................................................................
.........................................................................................
.........................................................................................
.........................................................................................
.........................................................................................
.........................................................................................

## Week Nine: Sweet Beulah Land

# Sunshine Night and Day
### WEEK NINE DAY ONE

"In this country the Sun shineth night and day; wherefore this was beyond the valley of the Shadow of Death" (p. 178).

"The city does not need the sun or the moon to shine on it, for the glory of God gives it light, and the Lamb is its lamp" (Revelation 21:23).

Christian and Hopeful entered the country of Beulah within sight of the Celestial City. The pleasure of the land depended on the absence of the Valley of the Shadow of Death, Giant Despair, and Doubting Castle. With assurance those places were left behind, they enjoyed the abundance of singing birds, sweet flowers, satisfying food and drink, and the coo of turtledoves in the land. They anticipated entrance into the City toward which long they had journeyed.

In Beulah Land (meaning "married" in Hebrew), the Pilgrims saw the contrast of the Bride and

Bridegroom as God rejoiced over the redeemed. "As a bridegroom rejoices over his bride, so will your God rejoice over you" (Isaiah 62:5). The Bride—the Church, the Body, the beloved—will meet Christ—the Bridegroom, the Head, Lover, our Redeemer.

**My Takeaway:** When teaching children the *Wordless Book*, I start with the ending: Heaven and what is missing. There's no need for sun or moon, and this surprises the students. Light comes from God's glory; the lamp is the Lamb of God. And this light shines night and day, with no need for electricity or batteries. This leads to our talking about what light means and how we use it. For with the guiding light of Jesus, we see what truly matters.

**Your Turn:** How does God's light, His Word, lead you in daily living? What are you looking forward to seeing when you reach Heaven's gate?

...........................................................................................

...........................................................................................

...........................................................................................

...........................................................................................

...........................................................................................

...........................................................................................

...........................................................................................

# Sick with Love

## WEEK NINE DAY TWO

"By reason of the natural glory of the City, and the reflection of the Sun-beams upon it, Christian with desire fell sick" (p. 179).

"Daughters of Jerusalem, I charge you—if you find my beloved, what will you tell him? Tell him I am faint with love" (Song of Songs 5:8).

Christian and Hopeful came down with what could be called love sickness, caused by the beauty of the Celestial City seen from Beulah Land. Its "natural glory" originated from the Lord himself. His kingdom shown with perfection as described in the book of Revelation: "each gate made of a single pearl. The great street of the city was of gold" (21:21). Soon they would go through that gate, walk that golden street, and look upon their Master's face. This thought filled their hearts with love and joy.

Two men in garments of gold quizzed the pilgrims about their journey and said, "You have two more difficulties" (p. 180). They would cross a river, not by a bridge, and their faith would determine whether shallow or deep the waters.

**My Takeaway:** Revelation 21:21 goes on to describe the golden street "as pure as transparent glass." In *The Great Divorce*, C.S. Lewis uses this to our advantage, describing how real Heaven is. The visitors step onto the grass and it's like glass, clear and brittle. They do not like its feel, for they are unaccustomed to what's true and real. While living on earth as Christ-followers, we begin to acclimate ourselves to truth and reality so we'll be able to welcome Heaven's beauty.

**Your Turn:** Does "love sickness" adequately describe what meeting Jesus will be like? How would you describe that meeting?

# Through the River
## WEEK NINE DAY THREE

"These troubles and distresses that you go through in these Waters, are no sign that God hath forsaken you, but are sent to try you" (pp. 182–3).

"When you pass through the waters, I will be with you" (Isaiah 43:2). "Death has been swallowed up in victory" (1 Corinthians 15:54).

Not eager to pass through the river, the pilgrims asked the angels for another way. Only two, Enoch and Elijah, had been permitted to enter Heaven without dying first. Entering the waters, Christian began to sink and cried out. His friend Hopeful felt the bottom and encouraged Christian not to lose hope. Troubled by thoughts of past sins, Christian struggled with his fears. Hopeful called out, "I see the Gate," and Christian responded, "You have been Hopeful ever since I knew you" (p. 182). Hopeful directed his friend to Scripture and Christian found ground to stand upon—his faith in Christ alone for salvation.

Two shining men awaited their arrival at the Gate as the pilgrims left their worldly garments behind, exchanging the mortal for immortal. They could hardly express the beauty of the City, the new Jerusalem, as they joyously looked forward to seeing and hearing their Savior.

**My Takeaway:** In *For This Day*, J.B. Phillips wrote: "'The icy river' is entirely a product of Bunyan's own fears, and the New Testament will be searched in vain for the slightest endorsement of his idea." Instead, the concept of sleep is used in Scripture. Personally, this thought gave me comfort in the early days of my marriage, for I didn't want to lose the joy I'd found. Jesus is my victor over death and its fears.

**Your Turn:** Many Christians state that they do not fear death, only the process of dying. What would you say to that?

........................................................................................
........................................................................................
........................................................................................
........................................................................................
........................................................................................
........................................................................................
........................................................................................

# Wedding Supper with Jesus
## WEEK NINE DAY FOUR

"These are the men that have loved our Lord, when they were in the World, and that have left all for his Holy Name" (p. 185).

"Then the angel said to me, 'Write this: Blessed are those who are invited to the wedding supper of the Lamb!' And he added, 'These are the true words of God'" (Revelation 19:9).

The welcome committee, the heavenly host, met the two pilgrims with shouts of joy, announcing they would attend the marriage supper of the Lamb. Trumpets sounded! Great joyous celebrations began with heavenly beings surrounding Christian and Hopeful who were filled with grand thoughts of what would come.

"Thus they were come up to the Gate" (p. 187). Here the pilgrims presented their certificates, akin to necessary passports of entry. How gratefully they had kept these with them the whole journey! As they stood at the entrance to the Celestial City, they marveled about their escape from the City of Destruction in contrast to the splendor now awaiting them. The King himself commanded, "Open the Gate to these who have kept the Truth."

**My Takeaway:** On the central stage at the Praise Gathering, hosted by the Gaither musical team, college students blew trumpets while men and women marched in with glorious banners emblazoned with various names for Jesus Christ: Redeemer, Son of God, King of Glory, and more. As I viewed this stirring scene, it flooded me with images of a heavenly host giving praise to their Lord and Master. What joy will greet us in the Celestial City.

**Your Turn:** Why were the pilgrims' certificates so important for entrance into Heaven? On what can you base your assurance of passing through the Gate to meet Jesus?

# Welcomed Home

## WEEK NINE DAY FIVE

"These two men went in at the Gate; and lo, as they entered, they were transfigured" (p. 187).

"His Master replied, 'Well done, good and faithful servant! . . . Come and share your master's happiness!'" (Matthew 25:21).

Throughout his book, John Bunyan wrote what he saw and heard in his dream. At long last he saw Christian and Hopeful enter the gate, "transfigured," suddenly wearing shiny gold clothing. The welcome home committee placed crowns on their heads as symbols of honor, and they gave them harps for use in praising their King. Bells rang with great jubilation! The heavenly host said, "Enter ye into the Joy of our Lord" (p. 187).

The two pilgrims, now inside the Celestial City, sang their praises to God: "'To him who sits on the throne and to the Lamb be praise and honor and glory and power, for ever and ever!'" (Revelation 5:13). The winged angels answered in chorus, "Holy, Holy, Holy is the Lord." In his dream,

Bunyan saw the gate shut, closing him out from the beauty of the city. He added, "I wished myself among them" (p. 188).

**My Takeaway:** Gertrude Behanna, a well-to-do woman of the 1900s, came to Christ through an invitation by new friends she'd met at a dinner party. Gertrude developed a love for the word "welcome." That word connects me with the pilgrims' entrance into the Celestial City. As we accept Jesus' invitation to follow Him, we sense a welcome party has already begun in Heaven. When we reach our heavenly home, we will get to hear that joyous welcome chorus.

**Your Turn:** What's so amazing about this welcome home party? Tell how you would imagine God's happiness over your entrance into His Kingdom.

........................................................................................
........................................................................................
........................................................................................
........................................................................................
........................................................................................
........................................................................................
........................................................................................
........................................................................................
........................................................................................

# Way to Hell

## WEEK NINE DAY SIX

"Then I saw that there was a Way to Hell, even from the Gates of Heaven, as well as from the City of Destruction" (p. 189).

"'Tie him hand and foot, and throw him outside, into the darkness, where there will be weeping and gnashing of teeth.' For many are invited, but few are chosen" (Matthew 22:13, 14).

In his dream, Bunyan saw Ignorance as he came up to shore. He had hitched a ride in a boat offered by Vain-Hope, so fitting that these two would meet. As Ignorance went up the hill to the gate, he had no one to help or welcome him. Not the least bit of encouragement met him.

Reaching the gate, someone asked for his reason to be there. Ignorance assured them he had rights, for he had listened to the King who taught in his town. When asked for his certificate, Ignorance "fumbled in his bosom for one and found none" (p. 189). The King commanded the two Shining Ones who had accompanied Christian and Hopeful to "take Ignorance and bind him hand and foot, and have him away" (p. 189). This echoed the words of Jesus who is our Judge.

Bunyan commented that even at the gate of heaven, there is a way out to hell. Bunyan awoke from his dream. But there's yet more to the story: Christiana and her sons will begin their journey in part two.

**My Takeaway:** I find it surprising that Bunyan ended this part of his story, not with the beauty of heaven, but with a warning of hell that awaits those who seek their own way. Christian and Hopeful enjoyed the presence of the King, while Ignorance experienced God's judgment.

**Your Turn:** As we end part one of *The Pilgrim's Progress*, what do you think of Bunyan's choice to include judgment along with heaven's joys?

# Part II
# Christiana Journeys to the Celestial City

## Week Ten: The Following

# Packed to Go

## WEEK TEN DAY ONE

"They all played the fool at the first . . . yet second thoughts have wrought wonderfully with them, so they have packed up, and are also gone after him" (pp. 204–205).

"To the lady chosen by God and to her children, whom I love in the truth—and not I only, but also all who know the truth" (2 John 1).

Bunyan had another dream, now about Christian's wife Christiana, and thus began Part Two of this classic tale. Since her husband's departure, Christiana wrapped her thoughts around the reason of his burden. Guilty about not going with him, her own sins weighed greatly on her. In addition, she stood in the way of her children's salvation. In a dream Christiana cried out with the prayer of the Publican in the temple: "God, have mercy on me, a sinner" (Luke 19:13).

The next morning, she shared her dream and intent with her four sons. With tears of joy they agreed to go with their mother to find the Celestial City and see their father. Visitors interrupted their packing. First Mr. Secret arrived and gave Christiana an invitation from the King; this would be their entrance into the Gate. Next to knock on her door was Mrs. Timorous, insisting that Christiana not leave because of the dangers ahead. Christiana and her sons did not change their plans but continued their packing in order to leave the City of Destruction.

**My Takeaway:** Like Christiana, my decisions have changed not only my direction but also that of our children. When my husband and I decided to move in with our daughter, it affected our grown children's attitudes toward us and each other. Not all agreed with our decision. As parents, our influence may be perceived as wrong, even though we deem decisions are best for ourselves.

**Your Turn:** How have your intentions turned around your own resolve and that of your family?

............................................................................................

............................................................................................

............................................................................................

............................................................................................

............................................................................................

# Mercy Came

## WEEK TEN DAY TWO

"Well, Mercy, said Christiana, cast in thy lot with me, I well know what will be the end of our Pilgrimage.... Nor shalt thou be rejected, tho' thou goest but upon my Invitation" (p. 215).

"Those who go out weeping, carrying seed to sow, will return with songs of joy, carrying sheaves with them" (Psalm 126:6).

Miss Mercy accompanied Mrs. Timorous to visit Christiana, but the younger lady had different intentions, at first hiding her change of heart. She said she would go a little way, but wanted to take the journey all the way. Mercy had no direct invitation from the King, so she was fearful, with only a kind invite from Christiana who was grateful for her friend's company.

While these started their pilgrimage, Mrs. Timorous gathered her friends to gossip about her visit with Christiana. As was Bunyan's style, the neighbors' names speak of character flaws. Mrs. Bat's-eyes, Mrs. Inconsiderate, Mrs. Light-mind, Mrs. Love-the-Flesh, and Mrs. Filth each had something to contribute by belittling Christiana and her journey. One said, "Good riddance," while another diverted the conversation to pleasantries such as dancing with pretty fellows.

While Christiana and Mercy talked along the way, they wept. Mercy felt sorrowful about those in the town who had no instructor. Christiana, while tearful about her past, found reassurance in knowing she was on the way and with her children.

**My Takeaway:** As a young mother, I claimed verses in Psalm 126 and 127 as my goals for our family. The Lord is the true builder of the home and our "children are a heritage from the Lord" (Psalm 127:1, 3). If we are to see our children saved, it will depend on sowing the seed of the Word by His grace (Psalm 126:6), and that can develop in several ways.

**Your Turn:** What promise have you claimed for your family?

....................................................................................................

....................................................................................................

....................................................................................................

....................................................................................................

....................................................................................................

....................................................................................................

....................................................................................................

....................................................................................................

# Follow His Example
## WEEK TEN DAY THREE

"We are come from whence Christian did come, and upon the same errand as he, to be ... graciously admitted by this Gate, into the Way that leads to the Celestial City" (p. 219–220).

"Blessed is she who has believed that the Lord would fulfill his promises to her!" (Luke 1:45).

"Follow my example, as I follow the example of Christ" (1 Corinthians 11:1).

At the beginning of their journey, Christiana anticipated the Way to bring many blessings before entering the promised city of delight. Arriving at the Wicket Gate, she knocked and the Keeper opened the gate. She confessed how she had resisted her husband's plea to go with him to the Celestial City. Admitting her earlier wrong decision, Christiana now committed to follow her husband's example. Grateful for a warm welcome inside the Wicket Gate, they heard trumpets and joyous music accompany their entry.

When the Keeper opened the gate, he did not see Mercy still lingering outside. Thus, Christiana began to plead for her friend. She is "one dejected in her mind," for she came without *proper* invitation from the King, only by her friend's word (p. 220).

**My Takeaway:** Soon after my marriage to Bill, I would listen to him play the upright piano in the parsonage as he sang from an old hymnal. Not only the words but also his joy brought conviction to my soul. I wondered what he had that I lacked. After one evening service, I asked Bill to stay after all our church folk had left. I prayed at the altar for God to "restore to me the joy of [his] salvation" (Psalm 51:12). God answered my prayer and filled me with His Holy Spirit.

**Your Turn:** Whose example(s) have you followed in your spiritual journey? What benefits have you received from this partnership?

..................................................................
..................................................................
..................................................................
..................................................................
..................................................................
..................................................................
..................................................................
..................................................................
..................................................................

# The Way In

## WEEK TEN DAY FOUR

"Mercy fell to the ground on her face, before him, and worshipped, and said, Let my Lord accept the Sacrifice of Praise, which I now offer unto him" (p. 224).

"Through Jesus, therefore, let us continually offer to God a sacrifice of praise—the fruit of lips that openly profess his name" (Hebrews 13:15).

Outside the Wicket Gate, Mercy knocked with trembling hand, determined not to be rejected. Two fears resided in her heart. She had no written letter, only a verbal invitation from her friend. Second, a fierce dog continued to bark loudly nearby. The Keeper opened the gate and saw Mercy had fainted. He lifted her by the hand and bid her "arise" and enter.

The Keeper gave Mercy the assurance she needed, for the Lord accepts all by whatever means they would come to follow Him. Mercy told Christiana her greatest fear was to be left behind. Christiana encouraged her friend, for her knocking indicated that she "took the Kingdom by storm" (p. 223).

Mercy wondered about her other fear—that angry dog—and asked the Keeper why he kept such a dog close to the entrance. Keeper informed them "that dog has another owner" (p. 224) whose purpose is to keep pilgrims away from the door. The Lord delivered Daniel from lions, why would He not deliver these pilgrims from a dog?

**My Takeaway:** Fear paralyzes us, and often prevents us from making wise decisions. Bill and I had left one town where we had experienced rejection related to our work. Several years later we accepted invitations to return to those same institutions. I told God I did not want to be that vulnerable again. With my focus turned toward God, He proved Himself greater than my fears.

**Your Turn:** Has some fear kept you out of the Lord's plan? If so, how did God provide for you?

..................................................................................

..................................................................................

..................................................................................

..................................................................................

..................................................................................

..................................................................................

..................................................................................

..................................................................................

# Forbidden Fruit

## WEEK TEN DAY FIVE

"Well, said she, my Sons, you transgress, for that fruit is none of ours; but she did not know that they did belong to the Enemy" (p. 226).

"You must not eat from the tree of the knowledge of good and evil, for when you eat from it you will certainly die" (Genesis 2:17).

Along the Way the pilgrims passed a wall where on the other side the dog was kept. The wall also hid the enemy's orchard, but branches of its fruit trees hung over the wall. Matthew and his younger brothers plucked the fruit, but only Matthew ate some. Christiana scolded them for taking the fruit, but she did not know the orchard belonged to the enemy.

It wasn't until later on in the journey that Matthew would be healed of his malady, but in the meantime, he hid the cause from his mother. It was "forbidden fruit," not only stolen but also grown by the enemy. This incident became a thorn in their relationship.

Then two ill-favored men came up to the women and made advances toward them. Christiana met their challenge with harsh but needful words, for she determined not to yield to their wrongful desires. This encounter could also be termed "forbidden fruit."

**My Takeaway:** While I have never had a man make an unwholesome advance toward me, I have read of such accounts of abuse. It's never easy to thwart the intended assault, nor report it to counselors or the authorities. What I've learned from those courageous women is that hiding the attack does more damage to the victim and society. As a Christian community we need to show compassion and grant protection. We can seek out opportunities to be agents of mercy.

**Your Turn:** What compassionate solutions are available for victims of abuse in your community?

..................................................................................
..................................................................................
..................................................................................
..................................................................................
..................................................................................
..................................................................................
..................................................................................
..................................................................................

# Christiana's Guilt

## WEEK TEN DAY SIX

"As for me, my fault is so much greater, for that I saw this danger before I came out of the doors, and yet did not provide for it" (p. 229).

"If anyone, then, knows the good they ought to do and doesn't do it, it is sin for them" (James 4:17). "For everyone who asks receives; the one who seeks finds" (Matthew 7:8).

Mercy thought they had left their dangers in the past, so she apologized for her heedless presumption. Christiana, on the other hand, assumed the greater guilt for she knew danger lurked ahead of them. When the two women cried out for help from the ruffians, Reliever came to assist them. Not only did the advance of the two ill-favored men lead to their discussion, but also they faced the fact that they had not asked for a guide.

Reliever asked why they had not requested a guide, since they were two weak women with children in their care. They had only to ask, and the favor would be granted. Christiana felt the guilt of this neglected request. A guide could have been appointed if only she had asked.

Mercy saw some good come out of their poor situation. With their faults clearly shown, they would benefit from this revelation. By sharp contrast, they understood their weakness and the Lord's strength. They had not asked for God's help, but His kindness did follow them.

**My Takeaway:** By experience I know being lost is frightening. Once I forgot to take an exit off the interstate on my way to visit our daughter. I stopped at a church and phoned my son-in-law for directions, giving him my location. However, I questioned his advice, and this came from a man who knew well the way around his town. My response revealed my lack of trust.

**Your Turn:** How are you with directions? What benefits are there from knowing your weakness?

..............................................................................................

..............................................................................................

..............................................................................................

..............................................................................................

..............................................................................................

..............................................................................................

..............................................................................................

..............................................................................................

# Week Eleven: Consequences and Victories

# Privileged Place

## WEEK ELEVEN DAY ONE

"We understand that this is a privileged place for those that are become Pilgrims, and we now at this door are such" (p. 231).

"Now the overseer is to be above reproach, faithful to his wife, temperate, self-controlled, respectable, hospitable, able to teach" (1 Timothy 3:2).

There in the Way, for the help of pilgrims, a house stood with welcome signs. Innocent opened the door and Christiana introduced herself, her sons, and Mercy. Excitedly the young girl ran to tell her master about the pilgrims who desired entrance. Inside, the owner and his family talked about Christian and even mentioned Christiana's name, for they had heard she was on pilgrimage. The house filled with joyful acceptance of the party.

Christiana called herself "hard-hearted," for she did not accompany her husband on his journey.

Now she's "convinced that no Way is right but this" (p. 232), so the Interpreter compared her to the biblical story of the lad who first said, "I will not," but later repented and obeyed (Matthew 21:29). Then Interpreter showed the company the rooms Christian had visited, all the while explaining their own specific meanings.

**My Takeaway:** In Paul's description of an overseer he includes the advantage of being hospitable. In this way the Interpreter's household excelled. As a Christian community, we can encourage believers and reach out to seekers of the Way. With a program called "dinners for eight," my husband and I have experienced wonderful fellowship times around the table.

**Your Turn:** What special times of hospitality have you hosted or been invited to share?

..................................................................
..................................................................
..................................................................
..................................................................
..................................................................
..................................................................
..................................................................
..................................................................

# Creatures and Flowers
## WEEK ELEVEN DAY TWO

"Now, said he, compare this Hen to your King, and these chickens to his obedient ones" (p. 236).

"Jerusalem, Jerusalem, . . . how often I have longed to gather your children together, as a hen gathers her chicks under her wings, and you were not willing" (Matthew 23:37).

The Interpreter showed the pilgrims around the fields where they saw a hen with her chicks. "Compare this Hen to your King" has a biblical interpretation, because our Lord wept over Jerusalem, longing to gather His people as a hen covers her young under her wings. This imagery shows what we would call the motherly side of God, as nurturing His children.

In the garden the guests viewed various flowers, contented where the gardener has planted them—another lesson for the community of believers. Lessons in sowing came with a warning about looking for the yielded crop. Each place they visited gave new meaning to simple aspects of nature.

Creatures and flowers revealed the goodness of their Creator.

At dinner the Interpreter asked Christiana how she decided to take the journey. She gave four points: grief over her husband's death, guilt about how she treated Christian, then at last a dream and letter sealed her choice. Mercy's story differed from Christiana, for desire to know the truth compelled her to go. That night Mercy went to bed "blessing and praising God" (p. 242).

**My Takeaway:** At one point in Mercy's story she said, "My heart burned within me" (pp. 241-242). This is much like the testimony of John Wesley, for he wrote, "My heart was strangely warmed." Our conversion stories differ at some points, yet we are all drawn by God's love.

**Your Turn:** How were you convinced of God's love and yet also convicted of your sins?

...........................................................................................

...........................................................................................

...........................................................................................

...........................................................................................

...........................................................................................

...........................................................................................

...........................................................................................

...........................................................................................

# Bathed and Clothed
## WEEK ELEVEN DAY THREE

"There they must wash and be clean" (p. 243). "Go into the vestry, and fetch out Garments for these people: So she went and fetched out White Raiment" (p. 244).

"Let us draw near to God with a sincere heart . . . having our bodies washed with pure water" (Hebrews 10:22). "In humility value others above yourselves, not looking to your own interests but each of you to the interests of the others" (Philippians 2:3–4).

The next morning, Innocent, following her master's instructions, brought the pilgrims to a sweet place for bathing—to wash off dirt from their travels. Not only did they feel clean from their bath, but refreshed and strengthened. This could very well represent the washing of regeneration. They also put on fresh new garments of white linen. These transformed their thoughts as well as their appearance. Each looked at the other and bestowed compliments, not idle flattery, but of true value for their beauty. They praised others, not themselves.

The Interpreter called for a mark to be placed on each pilgrim. This identified them along their journey, a sign that they belonged to the Lord. "Consider [mark] the blameless, observe the upright" (Psalm 37:37). These preparations readied the pilgrims to continue on the Way. But one more important addition: a guide named Great-heart, equipped with a helmet, sword, and shield.

**My Takeaway:** Throughout the Old and New Testaments, the Lord identified His people with the mark of His holiness, a sure sign of belonging. Often throughout Scripture we read, "so they may know that I am the Lord their God," and "they" referred not only to God's people but also the nations surrounding Israel. In revealing Himself, God did not include some and exclude others.

**Your Turn:** What "mark" do you possess so that others (family, friends, neighbors, even the world) will know you belong to the Lord?

..............................................................................................

..............................................................................................

..............................................................................................

..............................................................................................

..............................................................................................

..............................................................................................

..............................................................................................

# Pardon by Another
## WEEK ELEVEN DAY FOUR

Pardon: "He hath obtained it in this double way; he has performed Righteousness to cover you, and spilt blood to wash you in" (p. 245).

"Since we have now been justified by his blood, how much more shall we be saved from God's wrath through him!" (Romans 5:9).

All along the Way, Christiana was interested in the places where her husband had important victories or troubles. Leaving the Interpreter's house, the party "came to the place where Christian's burden fell off his back" (p. 245). This would be the Cross and Sepulchre. After this stop Christiana asked Great-heart about pardon. He said it had to be obtained by another, not oneself, for righteousness is needed for a covering and sacrificial blood for redemption. That question and answer led into a discussion about atonement through Jesus.

Only Jesus Christ can bring about full pardon, for He alone is the perfect God-Man. The Righteous Christ paid the penalty for our sins, and assuaged our guilt. Christiana rejoiced in "being pardoned by Word and Deed" (p. 248), for redemption came by the Word made flesh, who willingly carried our sins to the cross. Matthew, Christiana's oldest son, became an example of guilt being relieved. He confessed to eating bad fruit, which made him sick. Dr. Skill healed him.

**My Takeaway:** Before the pilgrims climbed the Hill of Difficulty, they met travelers who turned out of the Way. I admit shamefully that their names could suit me at times: Slow-pace, Dull, Sloth, and Presumption. By my inactivity or busyness, even at church, I could be an ineffective witness, incorrectly implying that salvation comes to us through works.

**Your Turn:** Praise Jesus for the pardon He has provided for you personally. Then give a witness to someone.

................................................................................
................................................................................
................................................................................
................................................................................
................................................................................
................................................................................
................................................................................
................................................................................
................................................................................

# Gave an Account
## WEEK ELEVEN DAY FIVE

"This Valley of Humiliation is of itself as fruitful a place, . . . that might give us an account why Christian was so hardly beset in this place" (pp. 280–281).

"He was led like a sheep to the slaughter, and as a lamb before its shearer is silent, so he did not open his mouth. In His humiliation he was deprived of justice" (Acts 8:32, 33).

Going up the Hill of Difficulty, Great-heart prevented young James from taking rest until they reached the Prince's Arbor. Aptly named, the hill made for a hard climb up but easier coming down into the Valley of Humiliation.

James pointed out to his mother a pillar with an inscription. Christian had left a warning to future travelers, for here he had a battle with pride. Although the valley bloomed with tasty fruits and beautiful flowers (depicting the abundant foliage in the Song of Songs), it could lead a traveler into self-centered thoughts.

Christian's greatest victory happened in a "narrow passage" where he fought Apollyon and won. Beyond that, he and the present company went through the Valley of the Shadow of Death. In Bunyan's dream we discover that these hills and valleys posed different threats to the varied pilgrims. Some were more frightened than others; some had a more difficult passage.

**My Takeaway:** Christian's journey seen through the eyes of his wife and Great-heart has given me a greater appreciation of what happened to Christian, as well as how it influenced others. I see here how I must be a true witness to those who follow me. This puts a greater responsibility on how I act and speak, for it's not only my journey, but how my life affects others.

**Your Turn:** Can you visualize those following in your footsteps? How will they fare?

..........................................................................................
..........................................................................................
..........................................................................................
..........................................................................................
..........................................................................................
..........................................................................................
..........................................................................................

# No Thought to Retreat
## WEEK ELEVEN DAY SIX

"But when he was come to the entrance of the Valley of the Shadow of Death, I thought I should have lost my man; not for that he had any inclination to go back" (p. 301).

"Because of the increase of wickedness, the love of most will grow cold, but the one who stands firm to the end will be saved" (Matthew 24:12–13).

New travelers posed quite a contrast: Father Honest and Mr. Fearing. The party awakened an old pilgrim from sleep, and ironically his name was Honest from the town of Stupidity. Great-heart had been the guide for Mr. Fearing. Great-heart and Father Honest described Mr. Fearing as a "troublesome pilgrim," who took over a month to get beyond the Slough of Despond. He seemed to be in sympathy with the Valley of Humiliation, then struggled greatly in the Valley of the Shadow of Death, for "he was ready to die for fear" (p. 301).

One persistent and endearing quality of Mr. Fearing evolved as he continued to travel to the Celestial City. He resolved not to turn back whatever difficulty he encountered. He never had any thought of retreat. When he came to the River, rather than miss seeing the face of his Master, he crossed over while the waters were lower than ever did Greatheart see for other pilgrims.

**My Takeaway:** I know that fear can cripple my spiritual journey. Like Mr. Fearing, my going through hills of difficulty and valleys of humiliation has often caused delays and even seasons of despondency. However, confidence in God's strength will be rewarded: "Persevere so that when you have done the will of God, you will receive what he has promised" (Hebrews 10:36).

**Your Turn:** As you rehearse your spiritual journey, do you associate more with Father Honest or Mr. Fearing or a bit of both? How so?

..........................................................................................
..........................................................................................
..........................................................................................
..........................................................................................
..........................................................................................
..........................................................................................
..........................................................................................
..........................................................................................
..........................................................................................

## Week Twelve: It's Not All Up-hill

# Lover of Pilgrims
### WEEK TWELVE DAY ONE

"Then was Christiana, Mercy, and the boys, the more glad, for that the Innkeeper was a lover of Pilgrims" (p. 309).

"Share with the Lord's people who are in need. Practice hospitality" (Romans 12:13).

"Because they were weary" (p. 309), the pilgrims needed a rest stop. Mr. Honest advised an inn run by Gaius (3 John 1–8), for he loved pilgrims. The party entered without knocking, for such was the custom for inns. The master of the house showed them to rooms, and when Great-heart asked about supper, Gaius said he would have something prepared from their provisions.

The cook's name, Taste-that-which-is-Good, clued them to what would be in store for the meal. Introductions ensued, and Gaius was pleased to meet the wife of Christian. Gaius went into depth about Christian whose ancestors first lived in

Antioch, alluding to where "disciples were called Christians first" (Acts 11:26). Bunyan took this opportunity to expand on the importance of Christian heritage, citing James, Peter, Ignatius, and Polycarp, among others.

Gaius addressed the four boys, now growing into young men, that they should follow in their father's ways and thus end up in Heaven with their father. Gaius also advised Christiana that she should find wives for her sons with the goal that more Christians might follow.

**My Takeaway:** As a young wife, I read Dale Evans Rogers's book, *Angel Unaware,* about her daughter Robin, born with Down's Syndrome. The book's title was based on Hebrews 13:2. "Do not forget to show hospitality to strangers, for by so doing some people have shown hospitality to angels without knowing it." For me, Dale's story provided lessons in love and acceptance.

**Your Turn:** What hospitality story has blessed you and your family?

..................................................................
..................................................................
..................................................................
..................................................................
..................................................................

# Favored Women and Weddings

## WEEK TWELVE DAY TWO

"Women therefore are highly favored, and show by these things, that they are sharers with us in the Grace of Life" (p. 313).

"In addition, some of our women amazed us. They went to the tomb early this morning but didn't find his body" (Luke 24:22–23a).

Gaius tied together his advice to Christiana to find wives for her sons with a hope that Christian's line would continue and multiply. He went further with application, suggesting that Mercy be given in marriage to Matthew, Christiana's oldest son. A while into their visit Mercy gave agreement and she and Matthew wed. To expand the advice, Gaius gave his daughter Phebe to marry James, another of Christiana's sons. Thus, two weddings happened in the course of their stay at the inn. Gaius stated the purpose was to have Christian's name remembered.

Leading into this talk and practice of weddings, Gaius gave a discourse to honor women in the Bible. He began with Eve by whom the curse fell upon the world, but then quickly reminded us that "God sent forth his Son, born of a woman" (Galatians 4:4). The list continued with rejoicing over the woman who washed Jesus' feet with her tears, women who cared for Him and the disciples, women who wept at the Cross, and those women who were the first visitors on the morning of the Resurrection and then reported to the disciples about the empty tomb.

**My Takeaway:** Gaius reminds me of Paul who preached about marriage and singleness, the advantages of each. As to the unity of faith in the church, Paul wrote, "nor is there male and female, for you are all one in Christ Jesus" (Galatians 3:28).

**Your Turn:** Write a tribute to a woman who influenced your spiritual growth. Then let her know.

..................................................................
..................................................................
..................................................................
..................................................................
..................................................................
..................................................................
..................................................................
..................................................................
..................................................................

# Food and Riddles
## WEEK TWELVE DAY THREE

"So Supper came up, and first a *heave-shoulder,* and a *wave-beast* were set on the table before them; to shew that they must begin their meal with Prayer and Praise to God" (p. 313).

"The beast that was waved must be brought . . . before the Lord as a wave offering. This will be the perpetual share for you and your children, as the Lord has commanded" (Leviticus 10:15).

The supper served at Gaius' Inn turned into a lesson from Leviticus as Bunyan used food to represent fellowship offerings. First the cook spread the table with a cloth, and Matthew got excited about what was to come, calling the cloth a "fore-runner" (p. 313). They laid salt and bread on the table, perhaps symbolic of pilgrims being "the salt of the earth" (Matthew 5:13). The main course referred back to the priests' wave offerings—the shoulder and thigh of a beast (Leviticus 7:32–34). This also meant a meal began with prayer and praise to God (p. 313).

Closing out the meal, the guests cracked both nuts and riddles. All riddles were answered with knowledge of Scripture, but "hard texts are nuts . . . whose shells do keep their kernels from the eaters" (p. 315). This provided merry entertainment as well as biblical lessons.

During riddle time, Samuel told his mother that he would like to stay at this "good man's house" (p. 316), and Gaius overheard and approved of the boy's request. The party stayed at the inn for over a month and enjoyed rest and Christian fellowship.

**My Takeaway:** 1) During a retreat for ministry workers, my husband and I enjoyed a meal prepared with food items that could be found in Bible times. 2) Riddles are often a favorite family pastime, starting with the youngest trying a hand at "Knock, Knock, Who's There?"

**Your Turn:** Recite a favorite riddle either remembered from a family gathering or a book such as *The Lord of the Rings* by J.R.R. Tolkien.

# Feeble-mind and Ready-to-halt

WEEK TWELVE DAY FOUR

"I am fixed; my Way is before me, my mind is beyond the River that has no bridge, tho' I am, as you see, but of a feeble mind" (p. 322).

"And we urge you, brothers and sisters, warn those who are idle and disruptive, encourage the disheartened, help the weak, be patient with everyone" (1 Thessalonians 5:14).

The innkeeper Gaius seized the opportunity to have Great-heart use his skill with weapons to kill a nearby giant named Slay-good, for he hindered pilgrims along the King's highway. Others joined in the search. For his own evil pleasure, the giant held Feeble-mind hostage. The long battle was one of revenge for those whom Slay-good had harmed or eaten. As with other giants, Great-heart won and cut off the enemy's head and showed it to the group.

Feeble-mind joined the party. Along his journey so far, Feeble-mind had received compassion from the King's servants. While he owned up to his name, Feeble-mind was undaunted in his resolve to reach the Celestial City. As the company prepared to embark again on their journey, Ready-to-halt, a crippled man with crutches, arrived at the inn. He agreed to walk alongside Feeble-mind who had reservations about slowing down the other pilgrims.

**My Takeaway:** Feeble-mind and Ready-to-halt remind me of the old song "Jesus Loves Me"––"little ones to Him belong; they are weak but He is strong" (Anna B. Warner). The psalmist, the writer of Proverbs, Jesus, and Paul accepted the weak, simple, and feeble-minded. I'm grateful when churches welcome those who are emotionally, mentally, or physically weak.

**Your Turn:** Have you known someone who is different, yet you welcomed that person into your church fellowship or small group? How did you and they feel?

................................................................................
................................................................................
................................................................................
................................................................................
................................................................................
................................................................................
................................................................................
................................................................................

# The End of Giant Despair
## WEEK TWELVE DAY FIVE

"I demand of thee, that thou open thy gates for my entrance; prepare thyself also to fight, for I am come to take away thy head, and to demolish Doubting-Castle" (p. 340).

"The King will reply, 'Truly I tell you, whatever you did for one of the least of these brothers and sisters of mine, you did for me'" (Matthew 25:40).

Great-heart was committed to "support the weak" (p. 325). The traveling pilgrims, weak and strong, recited their past experiences. Some knew Christian and Faithful and how they fared along the Way. For others interested in hearing their tales, the storytellers didn't leave out the failures of those noted pilgrims. Soon the party arrived at Vanity-Fair and found it different than when Faithful met his death there. Influence of those good men had changed the town.

A friend of Great-heart provided meals and guest rooms for the pilgrims. Mnason was his name (Acts 21:16), and he welcomed the company. Mr. Honest asked if there were good folk

## The End of Giant Despair

they could meet. Yes, so Mnason's daughter went to invite Mr. Contrite, Mr. Dare-not-lie, and others. They told the party that because of Faithful, now "religion is counted honorable" (p. 331).

Two more weddings: Mnason's daughters Grace to Samuel and Martha to Joseph. They stayed long enough to bear children. On their journey again, they came near Doubting Castle. Great-heart killed Giant Despair (p. 340), but before destroying the castle they found Mr. Despondency held captive with his daughter Much-afraid. These also joined the party.

**My Takeaway:** The company of pilgrims grew, and that's how it should be. As Christians, we are commissioned to evangelize and increase our number. We bring others into fellowship.

**Your Turn:** What story do you have about witnessing and leading someone to accept Christ?

# Ask and Receive

## WEEK TWELVE DAY SIX

"Mercy, what is that thing thou wouldst have? Then she blushed and said, The great Glass that hangs up in the dining-room: So Sincere ran and fetched it, and with a joyful consent it was given her. Then she bowed her head, and gave thanks" (p. 348).

"Whoever looks intently into the perfect law that gives freedom . . . not forgetting what they have heard, but doing it—they will be blessed in what they do" (James 1:25).

The pilgrims arrived at the Delectable mountains where the Lord's Shepherds welcomed them, caring first for the weak and then the strong. Where only tents had housed Christian and Hopeful, now a Palace stood. After nourishing food, the Shepherds escorted the party to view such sights as Mt. Innocent where two men threw dirt on Godly-man, but it didn't soil his white clothes. The pilgrims understood the reason. Mercy asked to see the hole in the hill called the By-way to Hell. There she heard prisoners moaning of their ill-fated destiny.

Mercy saw a looking glass in the dining room of the Palace and she wanted it. The glass had two sides: one that acted like a mirror, but the other showed the Prince of Pilgrims with the crown of thorns on His head and holes in His hands and feet. Christiana told the Shepherds of Mercy's wish and they joyfully gave her the glass.

**My Takeaway:** Various commentators have differed on Mercy's request for the looking glass. One associated her desire with coveting what was not hers to ask. Another captured the "joyous consent" of the gift giving. We could learn caution here about what we desire and what we should have. But remember, we are not to overlook the glass as a gift attached to joy.

**Your Turn:** Have you wanted something so much that it consumed your thoughts? How did your desire match what God wanted for you?

..................................................................................

..................................................................................

..................................................................................

..................................................................................

..................................................................................

..................................................................................

..................................................................................

..................................................................................

## Week Thirteen: Valiant-for-truth

# Sword of Truth

## WEEK THIRTEEN DAY ONE

"I fought till my Sword did cleave to my hand, and when they were joined together, as if a sword grew out of my arm . . . then I fought with most courage" (p. 352).

"Eleazar stood his ground and struck down the Philistines till his hand grew tired and froze to the sword. The Lord brought about a great victory that day" (2 Samuel 23:10).

The Shepherds adorned the women with jewelry, but gave no warnings as they did for Christian, for this company had Great-heart as their guide. They came to the place where Christian met Turn-away who, when he came to the Cross, turned back to his own town.

Next, they saw Valiant-for-truth with his sword drawn. He was in a pitiful state and his face was bloody. Even with scars from battles with thieves, Valiant had truth on his side, actually in his hand.

His sword never got dull, ready for battle at all times. Great-heart commended this warrior who fought against sin. The account of his journey included positive answers to three important life questions: "whose you are, whence you came, and whither you go?"

**My Takeaway:** We have come to my favorite of Bunyan's characters: Valiant-for-truth. It's how his sword cleaved to his hand that fascinates and motivates me. When describing the armor we wear as Christians, Paul associates the sword of the Spirit with the word of God (Ephesians 6:17), ever ready for action. I ask myself if God's Word is so ingrained in my mind that it's always ready, for I'm not to use it as an occasional word to prove a point. As my constant thought and life principle, God's truth is not a tool I put aside and pick up only when needed.

**Your Turn:** How do you view and use the word of God, the Bible, in your thought and practice?

..............................................................................................

..............................................................................................

..............................................................................................

..............................................................................................

..............................................................................................

..............................................................................................

..............................................................................................

# Shall We Know One Another?

WEEK THIRTEEN DAY TWO

"Since relatives are our second self, though that state will be dissolved there, yet why may it not be rationally concluded, that we shall be more glad to see them there?" (p. 354).

"For now we see only a reflection as in a mirror; then we shall see face to face. Now I know in part; then I shall know fully, even as I am fully known" (1 Corinthians 13:12).

Along the Way, Valiant-for-truth saw Mr. Tell-true who told him about Christian's journey. Thus, when he met Christiana and her family, he was overjoyed. That began a discussion about the afterlife: Will we know our loved ones and friends in Heaven? Valiant said, "How joyful will he [Christian] be, when he shall see them that would not go with him, yet to enter after him" (p. 353). Perhaps Christian would meet his wife at the gates to the Celestial City.

Then Valiant posed that question to Great-heart, who said Christian would find comfort when seeing his wife and sons. Great-heart stated that relatives are our "second self," and this was the logical reasoning for his answer that we will recognize family members.

**My Takeaway:** I'm fascinated with the discussion between Valiant-for-truth and Great-heart about the afterlife, especially the question about recognizing our loved ones. It's a mystery why Bunyan chose to include this in the dialogue and if he meant to persuade his readers. Their discussion, though brief, evokes curiosity, but we leave final answers in God's hands. We've all been curious about relationships in Heaven. What we do know from Scripture is limited to a few teachings in the Gospels, Epistles, and Revelation. Whether or not we recognize our relatives will pale with our joy over seeing Jesus Christ, our Savior.

**Your Turn:** How would you answer Valiant's question? What do you anticipate and why?

...........................................................................................

...........................................................................................

...........................................................................................

...........................................................................................

...........................................................................................

...........................................................................................

...........................................................................................

...........................................................................................

# Rehearsals
## WEEK THIRTEEN DAY THREE

"The Way is full of snares, pits, traps.... And that, after all of this, I should find a River [with no bridge] ... betwixt me and the Celestial Country" (p. 355).

"This is the victory that overcometh the world, even our faith" (1 John 5:4b, KJV).

Valiant-for-truth not only met trials along his way, but his family had put up opposition before he left home. We found this out when Great-heart asked about how Valiant started his journey. Having visited Dark-Land, Mr. Tell-true had told Valiant's parents about Christian's choice as a pilgrim. With confidence, he cited victories over many obstacles, but Valiant's parents thought only of the dangers. They began a rehearsal of Christian's journey to dissuade Valiant from going on pilgrimage. They emphasized pitfalls and disreputable people along the Way. But Valiant-for-truth believed what Mr. Tell-true reported, for only the truth swayed him.

The rehearsal of Christian's travels included dangers such as the Slough of Despond, the Hill

Difficulty, the Valley of Humiliation, and Doubting Castle. The report also listed those who either started and turned back or tried to convince Christian to retreat: Pliable, Formalist, Mistrust, and Ignorance. None of those influenced Valiant away from his right to be a pilgrim.

**My Takeaway:** Christian's journey seemed to be well known throughout the land and the account used for ill or good. Some, like Valiant, used the story as incentive to start along the Way, but others resisted and tried to convince their family not to travel. Along our way we can either grow through opposition or fall back into doubt and fear. Remember Valiant-for-truth bore scars from his battle with the three thieves. We cannot assume we'll escape scars along the right Way.

**Your Turn:** Write about an experience you've had when resisting opposition, perhaps from family or friends.

...........................................................................................
...........................................................................................
...........................................................................................
...........................................................................................
...........................................................................................
...........................................................................................
...........................................................................................

# Light the Way

## WEEK THIRTEEN DAY FOUR

"Then the Pilgrims desired with trembling to go forward, only they prayed their Guide to strike a light, that they might go the rest of their Way by the help of the light of a Lantern" (p. 362).

"For we live by believing and not by seeing" (2 Corinthians 5:7).

The party, led by Great-heart with Valiant-for-truth protecting the rear, arrived at the Enchanted Ground, a lovely name but dangerous, for the enemy placed it near the end of their journey. Although needing refreshment, they purposed not to stop at the Arbour, for rest might result in a deadly sleep, losing their way or falling into a muddy pit. It became so dark that they had to feel for the one ahead of them, not able to walk by sight.

Using his tinderbox, Great-heart lit a lantern and looked at his map to aid them through the darkness. The weary children cried out to the Lover of pilgrims for comfort. A wind lessened the fog and cleared the air. They came upon a man, Mr. Standfast, kneeling, with his hands and eyes lifted up. Mr. Honest recognized him as "a right good pilgrim" (p. 363). Standfast related his encounter with Madam Bubble, a worldly mistress. She offered pilgrims gold from her purse, her body, and her bed. True to his name, Standfast resisted temptation by running and praying.

**My Takeaway:** Often we are called upon to walk by faith, not sight, but we are never without a guide. We have our map, the Bible. Even when we are close to our destination, unhealthy rest stops may prevent us from arriving safely and on time. Having companions along the way reinforces our faith walk as we strengthen each other.

**Your Turn:** Write about an encounter you have had living by faith and how the Bible and Christian friends gave you the needed guidance.

# Blessings and Bequeaths
## WEEK THIRTEEN DAY FIVE

"Then she called for her children, and gave them her Blessing . . . . Lastly, she bequeathed to the Poor that little she had, and commanded her sons and her daughters to be ready" (p. 370).

"May the grace of the Lord Jesus Christ, and the love of God, and the fellowship of the Holy Spirit be with you all" (2 Corinthians 13:14).

The pilgrim band reached Beulah, a poetic name for the Promised Land, or as the song declared, "this is Heaven's borderland" ("Beulah Land," Edgar Page Stites). Angels awaited them with comfort and refreshment. Perfume and anointing prepared them to cross the River.

Pilgrims awaited their personal call from the Celestial City. They did not all go at once together, but left either one-by-one or in pairs. Christiana received the first call from the Master to stand in His presence within ten days, "in clothes of Immortality" (pp. 369–370). This gave her time to say her goodbyes. She first talked with Great-heart about their journey and next gave blessings to her children, proud that they had kept their garments white. After leaving her means to the poor, she asked Valiant-for-truth to watch over her children. She gave Mr. Standfast a ring. To the others, she spoke words of comfort and hope to see them soon. Christiana entered the river, arriving joyfully at the City Gate. Naturally her children wept, but their leaders rejoiced.

**My Takeaway:** I recall when my husband's mother entered her eternal rest while at our home. It was Sunday and she had asked me to sing with her from a hymnal. Later, when standing by her bed, I noticed she had gone, and I thought of the Scripture that God has set apart the godly for Himself (Psalm 4:3). Sadness and joy mingled together in our hearts and minds.

**Your Turn:** How does Christiana's entry into the Celestial City prompt you to make personal preparations?

.................................................................................
.................................................................................
.................................................................................
.................................................................................
.................................................................................
.................................................................................

# Journey's End
## WEEK THIRTEEN DAY SIX

"I see myself now at the end of my Journey; my toilsome days are ended. I am going now to see that Head that was crowned with thorns, and that Face that was spit upon for me" (p. 378).

"What we do see is Jesus ... and because he suffered death for us, he is now 'crowned with glory and honor'" (Hebrews 2:9).

A postman came for Mr. Ready-to-halt with an invitation to sit at his Master's table for supper. He had a specific departure date: "the next day after Easter" (p. 372). As Ready-to-halt entered the River, he anticipated chariots and horses on the yonder side, and thus left his crutches for his son. Next Mr. Feeble-mind crossed over with a promise to see the bright face of his Beloved. Of no use to himself or others, his feeble mind would be buried by Valiant-for-truth. A pair of pilgrims followed: Mr. Despondency and his daughter Much-afraid, relieved of their fears. They departed with: "Farewell night. Welcome day" (p. 375).

In a short while, Mr. Honest received his call and took his integrity with him. One Good-conscience led him across over-flowing waters. Next Valiant-for-truth left his sword, courage, and skill to any who followed. His "marks and scars" he kept as a witness of good deeds.

The last to join the party was the last to cross over. Mr. Standfast first asked Great-heart to inform his family of the delights of pilgrimage. Because the River was calm, Standfast stopped and spoke to those on the yonder shore about ending his walk by faith and beginning to live by sight. He focused on His Lord's beauty (p. 378).

Bunyan, the dreamer, closed his story with hope for an "increase of the Church" (p. 379).

**My Takeaway:** By including Bunyan's Scripture references, I've gained more from this journey with Pilgrim than reading Bunyan's book alone. This exercise has strengthened my faith walk.

**Your Turn:** What strengthens your faith walk? Use the next pages to sum-up your journey.

...........................................................................................

...........................................................................................

...........................................................................................

...........................................................................................

...........................................................................................

## CONCLUSION:
# Where Do We Go from Here?
### SUMMARY OF MY JOURNEY— MY TESTIMONY

I began . . .

..................................................................................

..................................................................................

I continued . . .

..................................................................................

..................................................................................

I experienced . . .

..................................................................................

..................................................................................

I learned . . .

..................................................................................

..................................................................................

What the struggles taught me . . .

..................................................................................

..................................................................................

What I enjoyed . . .

..................................................................................................

..................................................................................................

How I related to Christian and Christiana . . .

..................................................................................................

..................................................................................................

How I related to Faithful and Hopeful and other travelers . . .

..................................................................................................

..................................................................................................

Where my journey will take me . . .

..................................................................................................

..................................................................................................

Who I will invite to go with me . . .

..................................................................................................

..................................................................................................

..................................................................................................

Who we will meet on the other shore . . .

..................................................................................................

..................................................................................................

..................................................................................................

..................................................................................................

..................................................................................................

# Resources as Endnotes

**Quoted material for each day from:**
*The Pilgrim's Progress,* John Bunyan (2 parts), edition with Scripture references & notes by Bunyan, complete and unabridged, The Christian Library © 1998. Published by Barbour and Company, Inc., Westwood, NJ.  ISBN 0-916441-00-8
*The Holy Bible, New International Version, NIV* © 1973, 1978, 1984, 2011 by Biblica, Inc.

*The Holy Bible, King James Version, KJV,* Cambridge at the University Press, NY, no copyright
Quoted in Week 2 Day 1, Week 2 Day 2, and Week 13 Day 3.

W2D3.Rooms for Interpretation
Christopher Marlowe, *The Tragical History of Dr. Faustus*, from Quattro text of 1604, Hungry Point Press, Wabasha, Minnesota, annotated and edited by John Harris © 2018.
Louisa May Alcott, *A Modern Mephistopheles,* A Bantam Classic Book, New York. © 1877 by Roberts Brothers.

W4D2.Entering Vanity Fair and W6D6.Key of Promise
Alexander Whyte, *Bunyan Characters*: Oliphant Anderson and Ferrier, Old Bailey, London, 1893.

Voice of the Martyrs, a reputable resource about the persecuted church around the world. Check out two publications: *Global Prayer Journal* and a free magazine. vom.org   persecution.com

W5D2.Rich Friends in Fair-speech
*The Westminster Shorter Catechism*, 1647: "What is the chief end of man? Man's chief end is to glorify God and to enjoy him for ever." http://www.westminsterconfession.org/confessional-standards/the-westminster-shorter-catechism.php

W7D2.Within Sight of the City
Billy Sunday (1862-1935) was a national league baseball player turned evangelist. His baseball fame started with the Chicago White Stockings, setting a record for stealing bases. Born William Ashley Sunday, he was bar-hopping with friends when he heard a choir singing. Reportedly he said, "Boys, I bid the old life goodbye." Sunday, as an evangelist, had a unique preaching style, making his points by sliding into home on the stage.
https://www.indystar.com/story/news/history/retroindy/2013/12/04/billy-sunday/3871469/

W8D4.Flatterers
C.S. Lewis, *The Silver Chair,* p. 24, Harper Trophy, Harper Collins Publishers, © 1953 by C.S. Lewis Pte. Ltd.

W8D6.Good Use of Fear
John Newton, "Amazing Grace," 1779, public domain

W9D1.Sunshine Night and Day
*The Wordless Book*, Child Evangelism Fellowship, CEF Press. Order the little book or make it yourself. www.LetTheLittleChildrenCome.com

W9D2.Sick with Love
C.S. Lewis, *The Great Divorce*, pp. 27–28, © 1946, Macmillan Publishing Co.

W9D3.Through the River
J.B. Phillips, *For This Day*, p. 74, © 1974, Bantam Books for Word Books, Publisher

W9D4.Supper with Jesus
Bill and Gloria Gaither, Praise Gathering, Indianapolis, IN, 1996

W9D5.Welcomed Home
Gertrude Behanna, *The Late Liz, the autobiography of an ex-pagan,* written under the pseudonym of Elizabeth Burns, © 1957, Appleton-Century-Crofts, Inc., New York

W11D2. Creatures and Flowers
John Wesley, "My heart was strangely warmed." Wesley's journal entry for Wednesday, May 24, 1738:

"In the evening I went very unwillingly to a society in Aldersgate Street, where one was reading Luther's preface to the Epistle to the Romans. About a quarter before nine, while he was describing the change which God works in the heart through faith in Christ, I felt my heart strangely warmed. I felt I did trust in Christ, Christ alone for salvation: And an assurance was given me, that he had taken away my sins, even mine, and saved me from the law of sin and death."
– Wesley, John. *The Works of John Wesley, Third Edition, Complete and Unabridged, Volume I (of XIV).* (Reprinted from the 1823 edition issued by Wesleyan Methodist Book Room, London). Grand Rapid: Baker Book House. 1979.103.

W12D1.Lover of Pilgrims

Dale Evans Rogers, *Angel Unaware*, book title based on Hebrews 13:2

W12D4.Feeble-mind and Ready-to-Halt

Anna B. Warner, "Jesus Loves Me" – "Little ones to Him belong; they are weak but He is strong." Public domain.

W12D6. Ask and Receive

Commentaries on Mercy's request of the looking glass: coveting or "joyous consent"

W13D5.Blessings and Bequeaths

Edgar Page Stites, "Beulah Land," public domain

# Acknowledgments

Thanks to all those dedicated ladies who participated in the Touch of Class Bible study using John Bunyan's *The Pilgrim's Progress*—held at World Gospel Church, Terre Haute, Indiana. Thanks to Jerry B. Jenkins and his Writers Guild, giving me courage to begin and stay with it to the end. Thanks to Chad R. Allen and his Academy, coaching me through the process of a book proposal for submission. Thanks to all who proofread, edited, and encouraged me along this process of writing and book publishing. Most of all, thanks to those who have walked with me on this journey of the Christian life.

After receiving great care with the publication of three of my husband's books, I decided EABooks would be the best publisher for my first book. I'm grateful for the staff, including Rebecca Ford, Jeanette Littleton, and especially Robin Black who attended to formatting and cover design. Cheri Colwell, publisher, and Monica Miller, marketing, also contributed to the success of this work. Last but not least, I thank Erin Bartels for writing good back cover copy.

# About the Author

*Ann & Bill Coker–50th Anniversary*

Ann L. Coker received a BA in English from Asbury College, Wilmore, Kentucky, twenty years after graduating from Murphy High School, Mobile, Alabama, her home town. While holding the position of managing editor of *Good News* magazine, Ann edited lessons for Bristol Bible Curriculum. She contributed to *The Woman's Study Bible*, Thomas Nelson, Inc. ©1995, an assignment to write annotations on Numbers and Amos, along with eight topical notes. She has written for devotional publications such as *Pathways* (Warner Press) and *Quiet Hour* (David C. Cook). Her articles have appeared in *Celebrate Life* and *Lookout* among other periodicals. Ann has served as a client services director for the Crisis Pregnancy Center of Wabash Valley, Indiana, while editing and writing in their publications. She has led women's Bible studies in the churches where her husband, Bill, pastored. Their family includes four grown children, ten grandchildren, and thirteen great-grandchildren.